A GUIDE TO
JEWISH PRACTICE

FAMILY AND
SEXUAL ETHICS

A GUIDE *to* JEWISH PRACTICE

Center for Jewish Ethics
Reconstructionist Rabbinical College
In cooperation with the
Reconstructionist Rabbinical Association

Reconstructionist Rabbinical College Press
1299 Church Road, Wyncote, PA 19095-1898
www.rrc.edu

FAMILY AND
SEXUAL ETHICS

DAVID A. TEUTSCH

Reconstructionist Rabbinical College Press
Wyncote, Pennsylvania

Composition by G & H Soho, Inc.

ISBN 978-0-938945-16-1

2010903939

Printed in the U.S.A.

Contents

To my students and colleagues:
Your questions and insights
have challenged and deepened
my thinking.

Commentators

Lewis John Eron (L.J.E.)

Richard Hirsh (R.H.)

Leah Kamionkowski (L.K.)

Tamar Kamionkowski (T.K.)

Jason Gary Klein (J.G.K.)

Elliot Kukla (E.K.)

Nina H. Mandel (N.H.M.)

Dev Noily (D.N.)

Barbara Penzner (B.P.)

Steven Carr Reuben (S.C.R.)

David A. Teutsch (D.A.T.)

Sheila Peltz Weinberg (S.P.W.)

Advisory Committee

Rabbis Richard Hirsh and David Teutsch, Co-chairs

Rabbi Lester Bronstein

Deborah Dash Moore, Ph.D.

Chayim Herzig-Marx

Leah Kamionkowski

Tamar Kamionkowski, Ph.D.

Rabbi Nina Mandel

Rabbi Yael Ridberg

Rabbi Jacob Staub

Preface

How we deal with family and with sex has an enormous impact on our lives. How any of us handle them affects us, our families, our friends and communities. Therefore the ethical issues regarding sex and family have a profound importance.

This ninth section of *A Guide to Jewish Practice* continues the process of providing values-based guidance for contemporary Jews. It is funded by the Levin-Lieber Program in Jewish ethics.

The topics included in this book have proved challenging and controversial. The book has been substantially strengthened by the Advisory Committee, and particularly by comments from Richard Hirsh, Jacob Staub and Betsy Teutsch. The remaining flaws are entirely my responsibility. My assistants Cheryl Plumly and Raela Forman have helped with administration and word processing. Marilyn Silverstein did the copy editing. Jim Harris and G&H Soho ably handled the design, typesetting and printing. I am grateful for the intelligence, commitment and skill of all these people.

David A. Teutsch

FAMILY AND
SEXUAL ETHICS

The decisions we make about how to deal with family relationships and how to deal with our sexuality are momentous because of the power they have to shape not only our own lives but also the lives of the people around us. Those decisions have an impact on our own emotional, physical and spiritual lives, as well as on the fundamental building blocks of human society—individuals, families and communities. Sexual attraction and activity or lack of them, as well as their accepted varieties, play a major role not only in forming relationships and procreation but also in shaping family types and maintaining family stability and broader social stability. The broader implications of sexual activity should not dictate any particular stances regarding sexual and family ethics, but the approaches we take to each of these issues and to the responsibilities of communities should make up a mutually supportive whole. Thus, it is helpful to look at sexual ethics within contexts.

It is important to make fundamental distinctions between sexual activity, sexuality, sexual identity and gender identity. In broad terms sexual activity refers to specific sexual acts, sexuality to an inherent understanding of ourselves as sexual beings, sexual identity to how we choose to express our sexuality, and gender identity to how we see ourselves as men, women, transsexual, queer, or yet another gender identity. –L.J.E.

Family and sexual ethics must adapt to changing social, political and technological conditions. Given the fluidity of the current situation, it is inevitably the case that the issues raised by family and sexual ethics will generate controversy and uncertainty. Each of us witnesses considerable change over our lifetimes. This guide can raise important questions, but its suggestions must be viewed in this context.

Judaism is an evolving religious civilization, and that is the lens through which Jews have viewed all ethical issues, including those relating to family, sexuality, gender equality and the dynamics of male-female relationships. We are constantly challenged to adapt. It is a moral imperative to be part of that ongoing evolutionary process. —S.C.R.

Perspectives on Family

In contemporary usage, the word "family" has a variety of meanings. Some people use "family" to refer to a married couple and their descendents, while others include people who consider themselves a family even though their relationships are not legally or ritually recognized— "family by choice." While such arrangements can have important roles in people's lives, this *Guide* defines family as people related to each other by blood, by adoption or by marriage/commitment. Nuclear families are made up of couples or parent(s) and child(ren). Extended families comprise everyone related by blood, adoption

Our families are the first social units we encounter. In the context of family, we develop our self-understanding as individuals and social beings. Within the context of family, we learn how to share and sacrifice, how to deal with jealousy and anger, how to heal broken relationships, how to love others, and how to protect those to whom we feel close. As family members, we learn the limits of generosity, the obligations of relationship and the power of forgiveness. It is no wonder that scripture begins with an examination of family life before presenting the mandate and directives associated with the Sinai covenant. The stories of our most ancient ancestors illuminate the challenges we all face. L.J.E.

We hope that in our families we will love and be loved, support others and be supported, and cultivate compassion and respect. When this is so, everyone in the family can feel seen, valued and celebrated for who they are and for the unique ways in which they reflect the *tzelem Elohim,* the image of God. But for many people, including a disproportionate number of queer* people and people who have experienced abuse, our families of origin are not safe and nurturing places. D.N.

*The term "queer" refers to those who reject such binary modes as male/female and gay/straight in favor of a view that encompasses a great variety of gender identities and sexual expressions. D.A.T.

and marriage/commitment ceremonies/committed partnerships, regardless of residence, and they may include multiple generations—grandparents, cousins, aunts and uncles and so on. An individual can constitute a household, but an individual is not a family because a family by definition has at least two members. Households of various types can take on many of the functions of a family and may be treated as a family for the purposes of synagogue or organizational memberships or dues, but that does not usually make them identical with families.

People often create families of choice when their families of origin are unable to meet their basic human needs and they may have inflicted significant harm. Building a family of choice is a creative act of empowerment and healing. It takes a lot of energy to form and maintain relationships that, while primary and life sustaining, may not be understood or recognized in the larger world (workplaces, hospitals, synagogues). When we honor families of choice in Jewish communities, we fulfill the fundamental Jewish value of "choosing life." We celebrate people's resilience and creativity as they form families that affirm their holiness and bring healing and wholeness. —D.N.

The very essence of Jewish identity is rooted in the family model. We trace our roots as a civilization back to Abraham, Sarah, Hagar, Isaac and Ishmael, the first family of Judaism, and we often find solace by comparing our own families to the dysfunction, jealousy, favoritism and painful family challenges that the biblical text reveals. —S.C.R.

In pre-modern times the extended family was the primary unit of economic production, though of course it had many other functions as well. In such households there was only a moderate separation between the income-generating work and the work needed to sustain the household's internal needs. An extended family was an efficient economic unit, in part because children worked from the time they were very young. With the advent of the Industrial Age, the locus of work passed out of the home into separate enterprises, reducing the family's function as a basic, productive economic unit. With the increased mobility and affluence of contemporary society, and with the enormous expansion of the means of communication and entertainment, the family is far less of a center for social life and acculturation than it was a few generations ago. This is particularly so for Jews, who statistically are among the most affluent and mobile Americans.

As the functions of families shifted at the time of the Industrial Revolution, so too did gender roles. Work at home became the province of women, while men tackled the challenges of the outside world. This shift led to the advent of the first wave of the women's movement in America. In traditional Jewish family structure, this gendered relationship to home/outside world was already operative. Women were responsible for many of the mitzvot related to maintaining the home, while men were responsible for many of the mitzvot observed outside the home in the public Jewish community, including such categories as the mitzvot related to participating in communal prayer. —N.H.M.

In rural areas, farming communities and some lower income areas, extended families are still a necessary norm. —N.H.M.

The extended family has become less important in North America, with most nuclear families functioning independently. The rise of suburban living resulted in the breakdown of intimate neighborhood relations. With a postindustrial economy, ever fewer jobs require hard physical labor. For that reason and many others, the North American workplace has become much more egalitarian. As incomes in the United States and other affluent countries have risen, divorce has become financially easier, and households consisting of one person or of a single parent raising children have become more viable than ever before. The educational years have been extended, so that children are often not financially independent until they graduate from college and sometimes even later. The age of marriage has risen to the late twenties and early thirties. Women are likely to continue pursuing their careers during marriage. The number of children per family has dropped to an average of fewer than two per family. This may reflect the fact that raising children

The tremendous mobility of Jews in America has weakened relationships with extended families. One of the most important benefits that participating in synagogue life can provide is connection to other synagogue members, who become an extended family and serve as surrogates for aunts and uncles, cousins and grandparents. —S.C.R.

is a costly enterprise for families, generally with little financial return on this investment because most adults do not work in the context of their nuclear family of origin. The low birthrate may also reflect the facts that many more babies live to maturity today than in previous generations, and that family size now reflects the capacity to do family planning. Taken together, these sociological facts indicate how much the typical North American Jewish family has changed.

More Jewish households than ever before consist of a single person. While sometimes these households consist of young people who see themselves as not yet married, or of people who are divorced or widowed and see themselves as possibly marrying again, a large number consist of single people who choose to remain single. The affluence of developed countries makes it possible for many singles to support a household, and some people prefer their independence to the intimacy of shared family living.

Pirkey Avot (1:6) teaches that you should "Make for yourself a friend," using the word kana, which denotes both crafting a physical entity and making a purchase. Valuable new forms of connection are being crafted in contemporary settings to extend and enhance the traditional concepts of family. —N.H.M..

Married/Committed Couples

Families have historically had a couple at their core (regardless of whether there has been a wedding or a commitment ceremony). This partnership carries the primary economic, social, organizational, child-rearing and decision-making responsibility for the family unit. In the premodern, patriarchal world, the Jewish husband was obligated to provide a wife with food, clothing, shelter and sexual satisfaction, and the wife was expected to work within the household. This is the arrangement reflected in the traditional *ketuba* (written marriage contract).

In the emerging egalitarian world, couples are mutually obligated to ensure that these things are accomplished by shared planning, decision making, work and pleasure. Providing not only the basics of life but also the care needed when someone is sick, troubled or otherwise in need of care is an essential part of a life partnership.

Surprisingly in light of the progress toward women's equality in American society, most Jewish families continue to function with one partner (usually the male in a heterosexual relationship) fulfilling the role of primary income generator and the other fulfilling the functions of primary child raiser. —S.C.R.

Successful marriages are partnerships, and the best marriages are those in which both partners feel that they are actually better and more self-actualized as human beings because of the relationship. —S.C.R.

Life decisions should be based on self-knowledge and self-awareness. What makes us happy should, of course, be part of that understanding. But there are other significant issues when our potential happiness involves the lives of other people. Should we consider happiness the primary goal of life and/or marriage? Is happiness an ethical goal? — L.J.E.

Ensuring sufficiency of food, clothing and shelter is a necessity for good living, but it is hardly sufficient, given raised contemporary expectations.

The most emotionally satisfying marriages have feelings and acts of love at their core, not only at their outset but also through the years. Nurture, caring and support enrich the partners' lives. Of course the blessedness of the marriage depends upon the conduct of the partners. As Akiba, a famed second-century rabbi, put it, "If the partners act worthy, the divine presence (*Shekhina*) dwells in their midst, and if not, fire eats at them." (B.Talmud, *Sota* 17a) Marriage has never been easy, but the current high rate of divorce reflects both the challenge that sustaining a marriage poses in our time and the affluence that makes divorce financially manageable for both men and women. The hyperbole of some traditional texts should not preclude the recognition that some people are happier living alone.

The atomistic nature of American life and the rarity of multigenerational families living together have put an enormous and often intolerable pressure on individuals in relationships to fulfill all the needs of their partners. —S.C.R.

Extended family looks completely different to me now that I am a grandmother. When I was a mother of young children, I wanted autonomy and independence from my mother and father. I felt that my child-rearing philosophy and my outlook on life were different from theirs, and I wanted to be in a community of my peers. Now, I yearn to be near my grandchildren. It is a palpable ache that I share with many of my peers who live far away from their adult children. Has the world changed, or is this just the dance of the generations? —S.P.W.

The weight carried by a primary relationship has increased over time for several reasons. First, with most North American Jews relatively secure about having food, clothing and shelter, people seek meaning and joy in life, and this in turn has raised the expectations placed on their life-partners. We look to each other for growth, nurture, friendship, pleasure and companionship in leisure-time activities. Second, with the reduction in the intensity and frequency of contact with extended family and the local community, people's needs for association are borne more heavily by the primary relationship. In some cases people don't invest as much in their primary relationships as is required to sustain a relationship with such high expectations.

All partners must adjust to each other, so no two marriages or committed relationships are exactly alike. One of the keys to a successful relationship is clear and open communication. That communication is critical to negotiating task division, providing mutual support, making joint financial decisions, planning free-time activities,

If no two committed relationships are alike, what can be learned from the different types of relationships that the biblical patriarch Jacob had with the many women central to his life? In the Torah we read about the bond he had with his mother, Rebecca; his love of Rachel; his default marriage to Leah; and his partnering with the handmaids Bilha and Zilpa. Perhaps we can use these different relationships as a jumping-off point for discussing different kinds of commitments. Even Jacob's silence following his daughter Dinah's rape is a rich midrashic commentary on family relationships. —N.H.M.

deciding how to handle career and educational opportunities, jointly relating to extended family and dealing with friends and community. One of Judaism's key family values is *sh'lom bayit*, maintaining a peaceful home. Genuine peace cannot be achieved by papering over injustice, unhappiness or mistreatment. Couples have an obligation to be honest about their feelings, concerns, needs and wishes. Couples can thrive only when their relationships meet their needs. That contributes to *sh'lom bayit*, as does attentiveness to the needs of other family members. Supporting each other's growth and giving each other enough space to maintain other relationships and pursue interests that are not shared strengthens the primary relationship in the long run, whereas failing to do so can smother it. Sustaining a strong primary relationship is understood as a moral good, as is sustaining other relationships.

Avoiding criticism of the people we love is a great spiritual practice. How often does criticism have a positive purpose? Often it is simply a hurtful habit or a reflection of my own closed heart. Might I remember to pause before expressing every potentially hurtful word I could utter to a dear one? Pause, breathe and, in the space created, reflect: Is this necessary? Will this make a positive change? Will this serve our connection? Would this feel good if it were directed toward me? —S.P.W.

The value of honest communication and *hakarat hatov* (talking about good things) — in this case all the good things that your partner does — is clear. (See the "Ethics of Speech" section of *A Guide to Jewish Practice*.) Perhaps less obvious is the value of avoiding criticism unless it has a positive purpose that outweighs the damage the criticism would cause. On the other hand, impediments to a positive and mutually nurturing relationship deserve discussion even though that dialogue may be difficult. Counseling and couples workshops may be needed in order to maintain *sh'lom bayit*.

North American society has many examples of serial monogamy—of divorce and remarriage. On the one hand, no one is obliged to stay in an unhappy relationship, and one has a positive obligation to leave an emotionally, physically or sexually abusive one, since abusive relationships damage well-being (*b'riyut*). On the other hand, there is much to be gained by long-lasting relationships, which strengthen intergenerational families and add the meaning that comes from shared history and experience. Most relationships encounter times of stress, and with work they can often emerge stronger.

The rise of the Jewish women's movement in the last quarter of the 20th century correlates with a rise in Jewish communal awareness of issues of domestic violence and a rise in responses to them. Prior to that time, regrettably, this was an area avoided or even ignored within the Jewish and general communities. Many Jewish communities now sponsor specialists within Jewish family service agencies specifically focused on responding to domestic violence. Many synagogues routinely place information on domestic abuse hotlines and resources in women's restrooms. Often, educational programs about relationship abuse now take place in Jewish youth groups and summer camps. Increasingly, rabbinic seminaries include training in assistance and referral regarding domestic violence. The Jewish community has a responsibility to acknowledge domestic violence and respond to it. —N.H.M./R.H.

Like all relationships, marital relationships are much more likely to succeed if they are not overstressed. Living within the family's financial means, relating positively to each other's extended families, becoming a part of a community, and maintaining individual and shared friendships strengthen the connections that reduce stress on the marriage by reducing its burden of providing emotional support. Encouraging each other's commitments to hobbies and community service also helps to maintain a reasonable load for the marriage. Finding constructive ways to deal with aging parents and family members' illnesses is also critical to the stability of the marital relationship.

Although it may not have been the original intent of the biblical writers and editors, the story of Judah and Tamar (Genesis 38) and its placement in the text can inform Jewish attitudes about sexual activity. The ideal is a committed relationship; if that ends, the remaining partner is able to pursue other sexual relationships. For Tamar, after the death of her husband, it is another husband. For Judah, after the death of his wife, it is a non-committed sexual liaison. The biblical text makes no judgment about Judah's relations with a prostitute (Tamar in disguise) or about Tamar's decision to play the role of a prostitute in order to become pregnant by her father-in-law Judah. The problem comes in Judah's not honoring his responsibility to secure another sexual partner/husband for Tamar. Additionally, the story is a seemingly incongruent interruption of the Joseph saga. However, it precedes the attempted seduction of Joseph by Potiphar's wife. Joseph manages to escape, though Potiphar's wife punishes him with an accusation of rape. The two stories, read side-by-side, might be examples of appropriate and inappropriate sexual behavior. The actions of Judah and Tamar, who are both without committed relationships, fall inside the norm of appropriate sexual behavior. The conduct of Potiphar's wife, a married woman seeking sex from Joseph, a man not her husband, falls far outside it. —N.H.M.

Second and third marriages have powerful implications for those in the next generation. Many children these days have eight grandparents—or more. It becomes important as one of that multitude to remember how wonderful it is for children to have many people who think they are precious and special. It may be a challenge to avoid grandparent envy and one-upmanship, but it is important to remember that there truly is no limit to the amount of love a person can receive. — S.P.W.

In Jewish tradition, sexual relations are hardly limited to the goal of creating children. Family planning is a legitimate and important activity. Diverse methods of birth control are now available, and some of them can be used together. (For a discussion of birth-control methods, as well as one about abortion, see the "Bioethics" section of *A Guide to Jewish Practice*.)

When a second or third marriage occurs, the permutations of extended families, stepchildren and distant relatives grow rapidly. Marriage means family mergers, and wherever possible, extended-family relationships should be promoted and supported. We owe loyalty to our families, which are often a source of meaning and joy. Building relationships as fully as possible throughout the extended family will not only strengthen the new marriage but also help all members of the family to flourish. While minor slights inevitably occur in relationships, these need not become excuses for disrupting relationships.

Successful relationships evolve over time because the partners grow and change as individuals, and because many circumstances external to the relationship require adjustments. Accepting the fact that good relationships are not static is important in helping the partners to recognize and accept change graciously.

Serial marriages, whether as a result of divorce or the death of a partner, create larger and more complex extended families. They often raise issues of jealousy over the potential loss of an inheritance or the perceived loss of a parent's affection, attention and love. The more complex the family dynamic, the greater the need to follow Yehoshua ben Perahya's exhortation in the Mishna to "judge all people with the assumption that they are doing the best they can." (*Pirkey Avot* 1.6) When it comes to family harmony, attitude is everything. —S.C.R.

Partners as Parents

Most people have children within the context of a marriage or life partnership so that the financial obligations, rewards and challenges of parenting can be shared. However, not everyone has or chooses this option. It is increasingly the case that single people are having children— for example, through adoption or assisted conception. Jewish tradition regards having children as a mitzvah. The first mitzvah in the Torah is *p'ru ur'vu*, be fruitful and multiply. (See the "Welcoming Children" section of *A Guide to Jewish Practice*.) We hope our children will give us a future that goes beyond our deaths, a continuity that is an important source of meaning in our lives. The Talmud makes a pun between *banim* (children) and *bonim* (builders), for children not only build the family, they build the future of the community, of the Jewish people and, indeed, of humanity. (B. Talmud, *Berakhot* 64a) From this perspective, there is no distinction between being birth parents and adoptive parents.

Although the family unit has lost its economic power, the importance of building and maintaining strong and loving family relationships continues to carry moral and spiritual weight. As we speak of *l'dor vador,* from generation to generation, we recognize our individual responsibility to link our ancestors to the future of our families and our people. The bonds between parents and children, when attended to with respect and love, are often the bonds that individuals at the end of life speak about most with gratitude and a sense of fulfillment. —B.P.

Parenting often implies a partnership. Responsibility for one's children includes responsibility toward ones' partner and one's partner's extended family, even in the case of divorce or separation. —L.J.E.

Child-rearing is a demanding and time-consuming undertaking, but it can also be enormously rewarding. For many people, it is the most meaningful activity in their lives. Watching children develop is an encounter with the miraculous.

Raising children brings out an enduring love in parents that is often transformative. At its best, taking responsibility for a child results in maturation, increased self-discipline and personal growth that are hard to obtain elsewhere. People learn the transformative power of putting another person before themselves. As children go

Ecclesiastes 4:9 says, "Two are better than one in that they will have a great reward for their toil." If we imagine this verse describing a relationship between partners, then the Tanakh is reminding us that challenges in a relationship can lead to greater strength and fulfillment. —J.G.K.

through the many stages of their development, parents who are attentive to them develop as well. While parenting inevitably adds stresses and strains to the marital relationship, it can also create a deep bond. "Two are better than one . . . and a threefold cord cannot be easily broken." (Ecclesiastes 4:9,12) Reflecting upon the development of one's children and on the family's relationships often becomes a source of wisdom. Children deepen connections with extended family and create new networks of friendships that affect everyone in the family.

Some adults have committed, lifelong relationships with children to whom they are neither parents nor other conventionally recognized relatives. This is especially true among queer people, who may be less likely to parent children. Sometimes people use recognized words, like "godparent," to describe these relationships, and sometimes they create new language like "fairy" or "spuncle." Whatever the name, these relationships can add richness and love to the lives of children and their special grown-ups. Queer parents see such figures in biblical literature. For example, they note that Naomi had no conventionally named relationship to Oved, the son of her daughter-in-law Ruth and Boaz, her distant cousin. But she was seen as the child's parent: "A son is born to Naomi!" (Ruth 4:16-17) It is this queerly parented child whose line leads to David and ultimately, to the Messiah. Pharaoh's daughter plays a similarly queer role in her co-parenting arrangement with Moses' mother, Yocheved. —D.N.

In Proverbs fathers and mothers appear as teachers of *ḥokhma,* wisdom. The Bible reminds its readers that following the insights and directions of their parents, both mothers and fathers, is an essential part of acquiring wisdom. —L.J.E.

The Obligations of Parents to Children

The Talmud teaches that "a father is required to circumcise his son, redeem him, teach him Torah, take a wife for him and teach him a craft. And some say to swim." (B. Talmud *Kidushin* 29a) As people committed to egalitarianism, we might interpret this as saying that parents have many obligations toward their children — to name them and bring them into the Covenant (thereby making them part of the Jewish community), to teach them Torah, to help them establish themselves socially, to ensure that they receive an excellent secular education that prepares them to support themselves, and to teach them to protect themselves from physical danger. This list captures the profound Jewish commitment to learning and human connection, as well as to effective functioning in the everyday world. Clearly it is the Jewish parents' obligation to provide their children with Jewish activities and Jewish learning and to help them develop a Jewish consciousness. Parents may use the resources of religious schools

The talmudic sages discussed a father's moral and legal requirements to care for his children. They were not averse to applying public pressure on a parent who refused to take responsibility for supporting his children. To shame a recalcitrant father, Rabbi Hisda would stand outside the synagogue on a box and say, "Even the raven cares for its young, (see Psalms 147:9) but so-and-so refuses to care for his children." (Talmud *Ketubot* 49b)   —L.J.E.

The best advice for parenting is to be the kind of adult you want your child to grow up to be. Parents are always the primary role models for their children's behavior whether they want to be or not. James Baldwin wrote, "Children have never been good at listening to their elders, but they have never failed to imitate them." —S.C.R.

and Jewish day schools, and of Jewish camps and youth groups, but the ultimate responsibility for the formation of character and Jewish commitment is the parents'. If they do not model *menschlichkeit* and Jewish engagement, they cannot realistically expect their children to do so. The Talmud also clearly values molding adults who are capable of making their way in the world. Parents play an invaluable role there as well, not only by imparting concrete skills, but also by helping their children develop character.

The odd thing about the talmudic description of parental responsibility is what is not on the list. It contains no mention of providing food, clothing, shelter or love. How can that be? Perhaps those tasks did not belong primarily to the father in talmudic times. Perhaps the provision of these was not an obligation limited to parents, but something that everyone has an obligation to ensure. But perhaps they simply go without saying. It is hard to imagine caring parents who would by choice let their children go hungry, naked, homeless or loveless. The essence of parenting is providing the care, nurture and protection that a child needs so that the child can develop.

The Maggid of Mezeritch describes the concept of *tzimtzum,* the spiritual contracting of the self, in terms of creating a space for another person's growth. He uses the example of a father who withholds the answer to an equation from his son so that the child will have the opportunity to learn. — N.H.M .

It is easy to imagine how a loving and concerned parent can overprotect a child. To develop fully, children need opportunities to express themselves creatively, experience challenges on their own, learn the causes and lessons of failure, explore the world, and try on different activities and presentations of self. It is a parent's responsibility to be aware of the child's changing level of competence and interest so that the child has safe opportunities to separate, test and take risks. Younger children stay closer to home, both literally and metaphorically. As they grow older, they move increasingly out into the world. Loving parents set boundaries and rules so that their children will be safe and disciplined on the one hand, and have space enough to express creativity and develop on the other. These boundaries and rules necessarily continue to change as children grow up. Different parents have different parenting styles and expectations, so conformity to a specific standard would be undesirable even if it were possible. Still, some outcomes of parenting would be advantageous to any child. For example, parents who ensure that their children have good manners give them a lifelong gift.

Parents often adjust their parenting styles with different children. The verse in the book of Proverbs, "Teach a child the way he should go..." (Proverbs 22:6) reflects both the parental responsibility for guiding children and the uniqueness of every child. One of the most difficult aspects of parenting is the fact that being fair to each child may well mean treating each child differently, even in similar circumstances. —B.P.

In the best parenting, a distinction is made between punishment and consequences. When children have clear rules, obligations and expectations of behavior, and when they understand the consequences (both positive and negative) of fulfilling or not fulfilling those expectations, they are empowered to feel that what they say and what they do matter. —S.C.R.

Teaching children to respect appropriate rules and boundaries is part of how parents express love for their children. While children will sooner or later test the boundaries and sometimes become angry or rebellious in regard to them, parents can explain their purpose and discuss why the limits are where they are.

Parents' primary obligations to their children do not end with helping them to develop a positive sense of self and effective self-discipline. Parents also have a fundamental obligation to teach Torah. As the first paragraph (*V'ahavta*) of the *Sh'ma* puts it, "Teach these words that I (God) put before you today to your children." How do we teach them? Perhaps the single most powerful tool

One cannot develop a positive sense of self and effective self-discipline as a Jew without Torah – the spiritual, ethical and cultural heritage of the Jewish people. It is a basic obligation of Jewish parenting that parents raise their children not only to be good people, but also to be good Jews. —L.J.E.

Parents of the college students with whom I work occasionally call me with concerns about how their child is changing, Jewishly or otherwise. I sometimes quip that the best way to convey the behaviors we want our college-age children to follow is to act the opposite because children sometimes rebel in their process of individuating. All jokes aside, keeping lines of communication open and creating an environment in which any conversation is safe to have with one's parent might be the most important thing parents can do for their late-adolescent children. — J.G.K.

Yehuda Leib Gordon, the great 19th-century *maskil* (scholar) and Jewish Enlightenment thinker, urged, "Be a Jew at home and a mensch outside your home." Neither we nor our children can function as full human beings in a pluralistic world without a solid grounding in our own faith, culture and traditions. On the other hand, we need to enrich our Jewish home life by engaging in the best the outside world has to offer. —L.J.E.

is the example we set with our own lives. If I want my child to do good in the world, to study hard, to develop a serious spiritual life, to eat nutritious food, to develop a healthy body, to enjoy people and pleasures, to become a mensch, and to love the Jewish people, then I need to live in a way that models similar behavior. Almost as important as the example we set is the way we explain our conduct and tell the stories about our journeys so that our children can understand our choices and commitments.

If we want our children to care about integrity, we need to model and explain integrity. If we want them to care about community, we should not only model that caring, but also provide opportunities for them to happily embrace community. If we want them to invest in relationships, we should nurture our partnerships, family connections and friendships.

The relationships between parents and adult children evolve over time. Parents should support their children's efforts to separate and become independent, while at the same time recognizing that their children look to them for moral support throughout their shared lives. Children often turn to their parents for mentoring as well. Providing support and advice while at the same time recognizing children's need to live their own lives is a vital balancing act. It allows the renegotiation of the relationship as both parents and children move through the life cycle. At best it makes possible the emergence of adult friendships between parents and their children.

Sometimes it is important to explain to children why we are making certain choices. This depends a lot on the age and maturity level of the child. Clearly parents need to be sensitive to the "too much information" syndrome as well. — S.P.W.

The Obligations of Children to Parents

The Torah commands us to have respect and reverence (*yir'a*) for our parents (Leviticus 19:3). In the rabbinic Judaism reflected in the Talmud and medieval codes, revering parents means offering them unquestioning obedience — rising when parents enter the room and in all ways showing respect even when parental requests are unreasonable. In recent times generational hierarchies have become less rigid, and communication across the generations has become more open. Nonetheless, parents, who have literally provided life for their children, are deserving of respect. When children are dependent, it is reasonable for parents to make the rules and expect that they will be followed as long as they are not abusive. Typically more negotiation tends to take place during the teen years. However, revering one's parents does not mean offering them lifelong, blind obedience in the face of unfair demands. As children mature, they need more freedom to make their own decisions. Adult children should act with respect toward their parents, even when they decide after reflection not to obey them.

The biblical wisdom literature underscores the importance not only of adhering to the wisdom and insights of one's parents, but also of caring for them in their old age. (Proverbs 20:20; 23:22) —L.J.E.

Who decides if parents' rules are abusive? Children and teens are not necessarily in a position to judge. Because of the power dynamic between parents and children, the children may go along with otherwise abusive behavior either because they don't know that they are being abused or because they are too afraid to seek help. Other attentive adults play an important role in protecting such children. —N.H.M.

Revering and obeying parents affirms the value of what they can bestow—practical and spiritual guidance, Jewish and secular learning, and protection and support. While Jewish tradition emphasizes that we live in a world full of value and wonder, we live in a secular society where much of life is portrayed as value-neutral. At its best, revering parents is a path to discovering the value of Torah, the grace in the gift of life, the wonder in nature and the spiritual dimension of daily living — in short, to discovering meaning and value. Of course not all parents provide these things. But merely the gift of life — the minimum a parent gives — creates a debt with a magnitude beyond measure, for we would not exist without it.

In addition to revering parents, we are also expected to honor them (*kavod*). "Honor your father and mother" (Exodus 20:12) is one of the Ten Commandments. The rabbis understood honoring parents to mean providing physical and financial help when parents need them. In earlier times that often meant providing direct care in one's own home—which was often the family home—and

Honoring parents is central to the ten basic "commandments." As the fifth commandment, it serves as a bridge between the commandments to serve God and the commandments to live ethically among human beings. It is through our parents that we first learn to live in relationship with others. If we learn to show honor to our parents, then we can truly learn to "love your neighbor as yourself." (Leviticus 19:18) —B.P.

The distinction between respect and honor is a critical one in rabbinic thought: "What is respect *(mora),* and what is honor *(kavod)?* Respect means that the son must neither stand in his father's place nor sit in his place, nor contradict his father's words, nor tip the scales against his father (that is, if his father is in a dispute with another person, his son must not side with his opponent). Honor means that he must give him food and drink, clothe and cover him, lead him in and out." (Talmud *Kidushin* 31b) —L.J.E.

working to support the household when parents were no longer able to do so. With geographic dispersion, longer life spans, and better institutional and governmental support, the responsibility for caretaking has been substantially transferred to professionals. Still, personal care and supplemental support make a huge difference in older parents' lives. Honoring parents means ensuring that they retain their dignity, maintain social contact and live in comfort to the fullest extent possible.

However, the obligation to care for a spouse and children takes precedence over honoring parents if a partial choice must be made between them. The commitment to building the future takes precedence over obligations stemming from the past. People who are in the difficult situation of simultaneously caring for children and parents are often described as "the sandwich generation." They juggle emotional, financial and physical needs to help everyone to the extent they can. In these circumstances, it is also important for the generation in the middle to engage in self-care since equanimity and sustained emotional presence are needed in their multiple relationships.

Adult children have an obligation to keep in contact with their parents even when they are healthy and active. The children should look for opportunities for visits and shared activities, and ensure that their parents feel appreciated. In our time many adult children do not feel obligated to follow their parents' wishes regarding their careers, their leisure activities, or their family or religious choices, to name but a few. This reflects the high value that American Jews place on autonomy, an American ideal. Often a very real tension exists between revering parents and acting autonomously. It is important for parents of grown children to recognize the value of autonomy and minimize their demands and expectations on their children, while seeking opportunities to continue to be part of their children's lives—and especially of the lives of their grandchildren. It is very difficult to honor everyone's sensibilities, so it is helpful in ensuring *sh'lom bayit,* peace in the family, to minimize the areas where a parent insists on changed behavior from an adult child, or an adult child insists on change in a parent's behavior. The tension between *yir'a,* reverence, for parents and autonomy and respect for children requires thoughtful negotiation.

There are two exceptions to the obligation of children to maintain extensive social contact with their parents. The first is when parents are or have been sexually, emotionally or physically abusive. If the result is a relationship that is always painful, Jewish tradition teaches that children have an obligation to ensure that their parents' physical needs are met, but they have no obligation to have ongoing contact. For those who have been abused, this may be an exceedingly difficult obligation to fulfill. The second exception is when direct contact

---

In the Jewish tradition care for the elderly, just as education for the young, is a communal as well as an individual responsibility. The *Moshav Z'kenim,* the old age home, was a common institution in European Jewish communities and is one of the oldest institutions in Jewish communities in North America. —L.J.E.

is emotionally unbearable for the child because of the condition of the parent. This might be because of a parent's serious psychiatric problems, or it might be because of a physical condition such as a coma. This exception should be invoked only in extreme cases and, even when invoked, does not justify inattention to ensuring that the parent receives excellent care.

Relationships with stepparents are often complex. When a stepparent has helped to raise the child, the child has similar obligations to the stepparent as those owed to a parent. When a stepparent enters the family after the child is grown, the stepparent should be treated with respect and caring, but the child does not have obligations similar to those owed to a parent. In that circumstance, the relationship will dictate the level of commitment, reflecting the degree to which there is friendship, respect and trust. Sometimes stepparents have conflicts with children over the treatment of the biological parent or the amount of contact with that parent. When possible, the biological parent should clarify the questions of access and decision-making responsibility both orally and in writing so that there is no question of authority in cases of disability.

The need to juggle obligations to one's parents, children and partner reminds us of how crucial it is to see marriage as a partnership, a team where the two partners always know that they are the most important people in each other's lives. For a marriage to truly work, all other relationships must be secondary. —S.C.R.

Children who are adopted have the same obligations to their adoptive parents as they would have to biological parents who raised them. Children who had foster parents have obligations in proportion to the extent that their foster parents raised them. Children whose biological parents did not raise them should act kindly and supportively to them, but they do not need to respond to their needs, demands or wishes as they would to parents who raised them. When a surrogate parent or sperm donor was involved in the child's birth through a commercial transaction, the child has no obligation to that individual. However, if the child received such a gift of life without a financial exchange, the child has a greater obligation, though not one equivalent to that of a parent. Sometimes the surrogate parent or sperm donor remains active in the child's life, in which case it is the nature of the relationship that dictates the extent of obligation.

When an adopted child is interested in searching for the biological parents, the adoptive parents should help the child understand the risks and benefits of such a quest and should then avoid creating impediments if the child is mature enough to handle the outcome of such a search. When the adoptive parents are willing to help in the

As a congregational rabbi, I have often been asked the question, "How can I honor my parents when they have been (or continue to be) abusive?" Many wrestle with conflicted feelings about their parents and how to fulfill the mitzvah of honoring them without continuing to allow abusive or toxic behavior to infect their lives or the lives of their own children. Knowing that Jewish tradition requires providing only enough so that parents don't become homeless and starve is often very helpful to those with painful parental relationships. —S.C.R.

search, that may strengthen their relationship with the adopted child. Adoptive parents would do well to consult an expert in this regard.

For the relationship between parents and children to work, everyone should seek ways to communicate with warmth and gentleness. The principle *"dan l'khaf z'khut,"* "judge with the assumption of merit," is an important one for both sides in a relationship. Assuming positive motives, appreciating the gifts in the

Adoption, as it is understood in contemporary culture, does not exist in Jewish law. However, it is a mitzvah to raise and care for parentless children. Thus in Jewish tradition "adoptive" parents have more the status of a teacher than of a biological parent. The honor due to one's teacher is as great, if not greater, than the honor due to one's biological parent. Adopted children's searches for their biological parents should not be seen as a rejection of the adults who raised them. It is perfectly appropriate for children to know who their biological parents are. Ethical behavior takes place within relationships, so the adoptive child should take into consideration the needs and feelings of those involved in the search. Honor and respect due to parents and teachers generally take precedence over an individual's personal interests and concerns. —L.J.E.

I suspect some of the greatest experts to whom adoptive parents can turn are other adoptive parents who have been through this process. —J.G.K.

Yizkor, the memorial service recited on Yom Kippur and on the three pilgrimage festivals, enables us to continue to respect and honor our parents even after their deaths. Particularly on Yom Kippur, the day on which we forgive and seek forgiveness, a properly worded *Yizkor* prayer can be of great healing value to those whose parents were abusive. Forgiveness is not forgetting, but healthy remembering. Forgiveness breaks the hold of the past and makes way for growth. By reciting an appropriate *Yizkor* prayer, the abused now-adult child offers thanks for the gift of life and breaks whatever grasp the deceased parent still has on her soul. —L.J.E.

Parenting comes in many forms. The rabbis even suggested that one's teacher is one's parent. The sense of respect due to anyone who had a positive role in one's upbringing should be obvious. The more people one can experience as contributing to one's growth, nurturing and development, the richer one's life surely must be. — S.C.R.

relationship and withholding judgment can go a long way toward strengthening the bonds between the generations. Maintaining the connections among the generations is everyone's obligation—parents, children, grandparents, aunts, uncles, cousins and people of all genders. Together, they can ensure that everyone is treated with respect and empathy.

The principle of "*dan l'khaf z'khut*" is beautifully encapsulated in Rebbe Nachman's practice of focusing on the good. This is a serious practice that takes time to cultivate. The natural tendency of the mind, for self-protective purposes, is to seek out danger, disturbance and threat. Prayer offers us a way to focus on the blessing in our lives. How can we actually sweeten the mind toward ourselves, toward life itself and toward each other through seeing and accepting the merit in each moment? This is a worthy pursuit. Today's neuroscientists tell us it is possible to do – with intention and the right practices. —S.P.W.

Separation and Divorce

Many events can produce the breakdown in communication and trust that leads to divorce. While Jewish tradition encourages efforts to repair and revitalize marital relationships, there have always been situations where the rabbis supported divorce. For example, physical, emotional or sexual abuse would provide a compelling reason to end a relationship. One whole tractate of the Talmud is devoted to divorce (*gitin*). The relative affluence of North American Jewry has reduced the fear of poverty, one of the major impediments to divorce, and the raised expectations about quality of life have increased the frequency of divorce in our time. The trauma of divorce involves not only the parents; it affects everyone in their extended families as well as their friends. Handling separation or divorce in a way that minimizes enmity and disruption among the networks of relationships has moral value because it reduces the collateral damage.

Divorce often engenders anger, resentment and distrust between former spiritual partners. One of the best ways of maintaining ethical balance and fulfilling the mitzvah of *sh'lom bayit* even as difficult personal, familial and legal issues are discussed and resolved is for both parties to agree to divorce mediation rather than the inevitable adversarial relationship inherent in opposing lawyers battling in court. —S.C.R.

The anguish of betrayal, separation and divorce is poignantly illustrated in the book of Hosea. On the one hand, the first three chapters of the book serve as a manual on how not to do divorce. On the other hand, the text gives voice to the trauma of divorce and the devastating impact it can have on children and the community if anger and vengeance rule the process. —T.K.

Reaching fair financial and custody agreements as speedily and painlessly as possible is important not only to the couple but to everyone around them. While feelings of anger, betrayal and abandonment often arise in conjunction with a divorce, it is valuable to all concerned when these feelings are kept from slowing the negotiations or making them an instrument for revenge. Divorce usually affects the couple's children profoundly. The focus of custody discussions should be what is best for the children, who may be harmed by the divorce.

I heartily endorse the advice to divorcing parents and recognize how difficult it is in practice. It is unfortunate that friends and relatives trying to be supportive during a divorce process often stoke the heat of anger, victimhood and bitterness. This is not helpful in the long run. How might we educate ourselves and each other to be supportive in other ways? Perhaps we need to practice a similar silence to that counseled when one visits a shiva home. We can listen and hold the grief, disappointment, hurt, confusion and sadness, but we should also make a conscious effort not to fuel hostility and blame or offer a quick fix. —S.P.W.

Even after more than 30 years as a congregational rabbi, I am still somewhat mystified when I see divorcing parents using their children as weapons to hurt their ex-spouses or as leverage to manipulate the other parent into giving up equal parental rights. Parenthood is a sacred responsibility between parent and child that is independent of the hurts and disappointments of the spousal relationship that resulted in divorce. Keeping those relationships separate is an ethical demand and a spiritual commitment of parenting. —S.C.R.

Divorced people should be extremely careful when speaking about their shared past and each other. The temptation to speak poorly of one's former partner in order to justify one's position or to influence children and other family members is incredibly great. In cases of separation and divorce, one needs to be careful to follow the guidelines of ethical speech. If it becomes necessary to discuss the misdeeds of and disappointments with one's former partner, one should do so in a sensitive manner that respects all who are touched by the divorce. Particularly when there are children involved, divorce may mark the end of the parents' marriage, but not of their relationship and their mutual responsibilities to their children. —L.J.E.

One of the most challenging times to be a parent is during a separation or divorce. Parents under such circumstances have an obligation to see to the needs of the children — an obligation that supersedes the wishes of the parents. Maintaining a working relationship despite the feelings of anger and alienation that often accompany divorce is critical to the well-being of the children. Children need to feel secure that neither parent will abandon them, and to be reassured that they did not cause the split between their parents. Except when it is unavoidable, parents should refrain from providing information to minor children about their ex-partners' misdeeds. Divorce never diminishes parents' obligations to their children.

Interfaith Families

The number of interfaith families in the Jewish community continues to increase. Interfaith relationships can operate the same way that relationships between Jewish partners do. The unique challenges to interfaith families naturally occur around questions of religious observance and celebrations, both in the home and with extended family. Clear discussions about how to carry out these activities should occur within the context of recognizing the autonomy of the adults and the importance of shared family living. While this may not resolve all of the tensions, it is important to talk these issues through as part of the initial discussions about marriage, and to discuss them whenever anything changes for either partner in a way that disturbs the equilibrium.

Interfaith families are also intercultural families. Jewish identity formation consists not only of accepting Jewish beliefs and practices, but also of participating in the life and culture of the Jewish people. Being Jewish means understanding oneself as part of the extended Jewish family, including the embarrassing cousins and their bad behavior. The family of Israel is a root metaphor in the Jewish tradition. In an age when the primary understanding of the term "family" is the small nuclear family, this image — coming as it does from a world in which the extended family, clan and tribe had real meaning — may be harder to understand. —L.J.E.

I believe that religious consistency encourages emotional stability in children, a gift that interfaith parents can give to their children regardless of the individual religious beliefs of the parents. All children need to feel that they are loved and wanted by their parents. Trying to raise children as "both" puts them in the no-win emotional position of having to constantly juggle. Children in this kind of situation feel pressure to make sure they don't make either parent feel betrayed, and they act out of fear that as a result of their conduct, one parent or the other might withdraw his or her love. —S.C.R.

Agreements between partners about the religious up-bringing of children should be as explicit and detailed as possible. Some children are raised without any religion; some are raised in two religions; some are raised in one with some exposure to another; and some are raised exclusively in one. It is not fair to children to expose them to more than one religious tradition and then expect them to choose. Such exposure does not provide the depth of experience and knowledge of Judaism or another religion that would allow a child to make a meaningful choice. Since choosing a religion is a form of identifying with one parent and rejecting the other, this expectation creates a cruel conundrum for the child.

When parents are confused about religion in the home, their children are confused, but when parents are clear and explicit about their religious expectations of each other and of their children, this provides a safe emotional context in which religion can play a positive role in children's lives.   —S.C.R.

When I was the rabbi of a congregation, I was unsure what to call someone who was not Jewish and was raising a Jewish child. Here is a person who is part of a Jewish family and community, committed to the future of the Jewish people. I think we need a new term for such a person. Could it be "Jew by family" as opposed to "Jew by choice"?   —S.P.W.

Many members of the Jewish community—people who are partnered with Jews and who are, in many cases, raising their children as Jewish—come from religious families of origin outside the Jewish community. The existence of this growing group alerts us to the need to find an alternative to the term "non-Jew." But a commitment to inclusivity and welcoming can sometimes run ahead of other issues that need to be considered. For example, some have experimented with conferring the title *ger toshav* (based on the biblical "resident stranger") on people of other faith backgrounds or affirmations. Doing so can overlook whether that is something wanted by, appropriate to, or meaningful to them. It also overlooks the question of whether such a term would be comprehensible beyond an individual Jewish community.

Increasingly, non-Jewish parents play major roles in raising their children as Jews, a reality that deserves respect and support from both family members and the broader Jewish community. Sometimes the non-Jewish partner decides to convert to Judaism long after the marriage has taken place. Regardless of whether that occurs or not, the partner raising a Jewish child should receive appreciation and respect.

It is helpful to distinguish between "name" and "status." We need to find a positive, independent nomenclature to replace "non-Jew" that does not start with an image of "the other" and is not self-referential ("us and not us"). That should not mean conferring a status within the Jewish community that confuses the real distinction between people who are Jewish and those who are not. As the demographics of the Jewish community continue to change, we can expect to see experiments, suggestions and alternatives before a consensus emerges about the best term for people of other faith backgrounds and/or current affirmations who are partnered with Jews and participating in the life of the Jewish people.   —R.H.

Many intermarried parents are what I call "Jews by association" — individuals who may never convert but who have chosen to cast their lot with the Jewish people and who are thoroughly a part of what we understand to be 21st-century Jewish civilization. —S.C.R.

The stories of our people's origins include many non-Jewish (non-Israelite) family members who play positive roles. The Moabite woman Ruth chooses to make a lifelong commitment to Naomi, her Israelite mother-in-law. In so doing, Ruth becomes the progenitor of King David, from whose line the messiah will come. Ultimately, the future vision of a utopian world begins with one woman's attachment to and love for a Jewish relative. —T.K.

The Changing World of Sexuality

Improvements in healthcare and reproductive technology have led to many changes in the relationship between sexuality and childbearing. Two phenomena are worth special consideration. First, the development of effective birth control methods has allowed heterosexual couples to share vaginal intercourse with a low likelihood of pregnancy. Second, with the advent of donor insemination, it has become possible for a woman to bear a child without having a sexual relationship with a man. As a result of these two major changes, decisions about sexual activity have become separated from decisions about having children to an extent unimaginable just a few generations ago. Coupled with a shift in the way some of us think about *p'ru ur'vu,* the biblical commandment to be fruitful and multiply (Genesis 1:28), as a result of increased concern about overpopulation, sexual activity is more detached from procreation than ever before.

Patriarchy shaped most of sexual life in the Western world until relatively recently. One aspect of patriarchy is the male desire to control women's sex lives so that men can be certain of the parentage of their children and heirs. As a result, Jewish tradition from biblical times onward usually placed an emphasis on the value of female

In spite of the tremendous advances in reproductive technology and the reality that sexual activity can come without risk of pregnancy for both men and women, traditional stereotypes with different gender expectations still persist in our culture. This is evidenced by teenage boys being extolled as "studs" and teenage girls being denigrated as "sluts" when they engage in exactly the same sexual behavior. —S.C.R.

virginity but not on male virginity, on female fidelity but not on male fidelity. Today women's increased economic and social independence, coupled with the scientific means to document paternity, has fostered much greater equality in sexual relations. The later average date of marriage and the availability of sophisticated methods of contraception have resulted in women's increased sexual activity prior to marriage. Virginity at the time of marriage, once assumed by the rabbis, is much less common today.

All these shifts affect not only sexual relationships between men and women, but also attitudes toward homosexuality and bisexuality, as well as toward gender identity. The structural constraints on the expression of homosexuality, bisexuality and non-binary gender construction are considerably diminished for several reasons: accidental pregnancy is much less of an issue; adoption, abortion and donor insemination are available; and gender roles are less pronounced because of broad social and economic change.

The concept of sexuality is a modern idea. In biblical and Hellenistic cultures, people were not seen as sexual beings whose sexual lives expressed part of their unique inner core. Rather, people were seen as sexual actors, beings who perform certain sexual acts, some of which are proper and others improper or even forbidden. This fundamental difference in understanding the human psyche makes it difficult to translate pre-modern approaches to sexual activity to contemporary notions of sexuality. —L.J.E.

In spite of how far our society has progressed over the thousands of years of Jewish life, the amount of sexual coercion found in nearly every type of work environment continues to be a major source of emotional anxiety and pressure, particularly for women. In addition, when economic times are at their most difficult, sexual exploitation becomes easier to get away with in the workplace. — S.C.R.

Sexual Pleasure

One thing that has not changed regarding sexual activity is that it is still primarily motivated by the quest for pleasure. Sexual pleasure involves a number of aspects, such as sensuality, intimacy, play, fantasy and orgasm. Traditionally permitted activities for married couples include all possible modes of touching, all positions for sexual intercourse, and oral and anal sex. Sexual pleasure has always been appreciated within Jewish tradition, which is why the right to conjugal pleasure, *ona,* was a carefully delineated aspect of biblical and rabbinic law regarding marriage (Exodus 21:10). Due to the value placed on health, acts that cause injury are prohibited, as are those that are unwelcome to one of the partners. The initiating partner should seek clear, voluntary consent before proceeding. Either partner has the right to stop a sexual activity at any time.

The sexual act can bring sublime pleasure. In the Talmud (*Berakhot* 57b) marital sexual intercourse, along with Shabbat and a sunny day, are described as offering a small sample of the bliss of the world to come. Yet pleasure itself is at best a byproduct and not a goal of Jewish ethical and spiritual practice. The aim is to manifest *kedusha,* holiness, in this world by following Torah, as expressed through the traditions of Israel, in pursuit of *tzedeka*/justice, *hesed*/compassion and *shalom*/wholeness. The guiding principle is *hokhma*/wisdom and not pleasure. Pleasure lies in the realm of the impulses that push us off the straight path. Ritually, through a system of *b'rakhot*/blessings, we can utilize the energy of these impulses to produce *kedusha.* In the marriage ceremony, the blessing of *erusin*/sanctification acknowledges the potential for *kedusha* in marital intimacy, in much the same way as the Friday night kiddush acknowledges the experience of kedusha that wine and feasting can produce. —L.J.E.

Jewish tradition recognizes the right of married couples to engage in any mutually agreeable form of sexual activity so long as it does not result in *hashhatat zera,* the intentional spilling of semen that wastes an opportunity to create new life. In contemporary times, liberal authorities have interpreted the concern with *hashhatat zera,* which has its roots in the story of Onan (Genesis 38:7-10), to be limited to preventing pregnancy in violation of an agreement between spouses that they will attempt to become pregnant. Today any remaining concern about *hashhatat zera* has taken a back seat to an appreciation of the pleasure associated with male masturbation, as well as to the imperative to use a condom to prevent the spread of sexually transmitted diseases (STDs). Jewish tradition never banned female masturbation, since it involves no issue of seminal discharge. Thus, all forms of autoeroticism are permitted. Masturbation is a legitimate source of pleasure and of physical release, and it is far better than an inappropriate sexual partnership.

There is truly no such thing as "safe sex." Sexual intercourse means opening oneself to another in the most intimate way. It means taking a chance with another person. It means risking being hurt or being used. While people can perform any number of sexual acts, there is a difference between engaging in sexual activity in order to achieve physical pleasure, an orgasm, in which only the physical aspect of our being is engaged, and sharing sexual intimacy as a way of bonding with another human being that involves our entire physical and spiritual being. The institution of marriage provides a socially accepted structure in which the emotional and spiritual risks involved in true lovemaking are mitigated. —L.J.E.

Jewish tradition recognizes that sexual activity has the potential to bind partners together and increase their sense of intimacy. The medieval text *Iggeret Hakodesh, The Holy Letter*, often erroneously ascribed to Ramban (a 13th-century philosopher and Bible commentator), emphasizes that marital sexual activity is sacred when done with awareness that intimacy has a divine aspect to it. Such holiness is possible only when there is no coercion, when the relationship is legitimate, and when the lovers are attentive to each other's needs and wishes. This aspect of sexual activity does not apply to casual sexual relationships that lack an ongoing mutual commitment.

Sexual activity obviously does not need to be limited to times when people want to conceive a child. Sexual pleasure is desirable. Partners who know that they are unable to conceive a child can still delight in sexual activity. The primary questions around sexual activity are with whom it should take place and under what circumstances.

Prohibited Sexual Partners

Incest (sexual relations between members of the same family) is prohibited for many reasons. One obvious reason is the increased danger of genetic defects as a result of inbreeding. At least as important is the reality that families work best when they are characterized by intimacy and safety. If family members were likely to be the subjects of sexual advances, all kinds of intimacy between family members would be unsafe. Unwanted sex is likely to be deeply damaging emotionally. For sexual activity to be legitimate, the consent of the partners must be freely given. Children do not have the knowledge, experience or maturity to give free consent, so sexual relationships with minors (pedophilia and pederasty) are always forbidden. They are exploitative and often leave life-long damage.

Since families are characterized by complex power relations, those who are approached for sex by family members by definition cannot give free consent. What about incest between consenting adults who are either of the same sex or who carefully take contraceptive measures? In that case, the danger lies not in the sexual activity itself but in the precedent it might set — a precedent that would have the effect of making it easier for other kinds of incest to occur. A long list of the forbidden degrees of incest can be found in Leviticus 20:11-21. Cousins are not

Curiously, the Leviticus verses do not mention father-daughter incest explicitly. Rabbinic tradition points out that this is obvious from the context, but it is important to notice this irony when we are seeking to help survivors feel empowered through ancient texts and they discover that this most common form of abuse is unmentioned. —J.G.K.

prohibited from having a sexual relationship or marrying, but everyone more closely related than that is barred. Relatives who are adopted or who are step-siblings with no blood relationship are not prohibited by Jewish tradition from having a sexual relationship, but if they have ever lived as brother or sister in the same household, the issues of coercion and the undermining of safe intimacy suggest that such sexual relationships should be avoided. Even where such relationships are freely entered into, they can severely damage other familial relations if they should go awry. The risk is not acceptable in contemporary ethical terms or according to traditional Jewish precepts.

Many professional relationships require a level of safety and emotional intimacy that is possible only when very clear boundaries are maintained. For example, therapists, social workers, clergy, professors and teachers have an obligation, by virtue of their roles, to avoid both romantic involvement and sexual contact with their students, clients and congregants. Many believe that even long after the professional relationship has ended, a sexual and/or romantic relationship between such individuals remains improper. At the very least, once the professional relationship has officially ended, a considerable amount of time ought to elapse before the professional, whose job it is to maintain boundaries, allows the nature of the relationship to change.

Some people have power over each other, such as supervisors vis-à-vis employees, teachers vis-à-vis students, and lenders vis-à-vis borrowers. This creates the possibility that coercion may be a factor in any sexual or romantic relationship that occurs between them. The issue of potential coercion should be carefully explored, preferably with the help of an outside counseling professional, before a relationship starts. If that does not occur, the possibility of the coercive element corrupting the relationship is significant. Any element of coercion in a sexual relationship is prohibited, for it treats the sexual partner as an object to be exploited instead of as an equal partner. For the same reason, seduction or sexual activity for the purpose of economic, political or professional advancement is unethical.

Another example of a prohibited relationship is one that is coerced by violence or the threat of violence. Such coercion is illegal and immoral. It can do enormous harm, creating deep trauma that can last a lifetime. Whether in the form of spousal abuse, the rape of a stranger or a refusal to take no for an answer during a date, the use of force is a denial of the fact that human beings are made *b'tzelem Elohim,* in the image of God. Using any form of coercion or force is a violation of the fundamental *kavod,* the dignity that is every human being's due.

Sexual Activity:
When, What and with Whom

A broad array of sexual choices confronts people from their early teenage years onward, and the personal, familial and social impact of these choices is enormous. Sexual activity can run the range from holding hands to passionate lovemaking. Sexual activity can affirm the bond between people, or it can be objectifying and depersonalizing. Within the very wide range of permitted sexual activity, how does one decide what one ought to do?

The ideal context for sexual activity is a sanctified, committed partnership characterized by *ahava* (love), *emet* (fidelity), and *kedusha* (holiness). In such a relationship, each person would see a reflection of the divine (*tzelem Elohim*) in the other, and the sexual relationship would be a source of *simḥa* (joy), *kavod* (honor, dignity) and *sh'lom bayit* (peace in the home). Of course, mutually pleasurable sexual activity can also take place in situations far short of that ideal.

Two major factors are the maturity and experience of the individuals involved. More intimate sexual activities involve greater intensity and vulnerability and therefore should take place when people are more mature. Another factor is the stage of the relationship. When people have come to know each other better and have developed a more significant emotional bond, intimate sexual activity has a more natural context. Other factors are the communication and resulting understanding about the significance of the sexual activity and the relationship between the people involved. Thoughtful communication avoids misunderstandings and unnecessary conflicts. In making decisions about sexual activity, one is responsible not only for protecting oneself; one is also responsible for the well-being of one's partner.

Jewish tradition places a strong emphasis on *b'riyut* (health) and *sh'mirat haguf* (protecting the body). Some STDs, such as HIV/AIDS, can be life-threatening, and others, such as genital herpes, are life-affecting. Genital warts can lead to infertility. In light of this reality, the imperative to observe health precautions takes on critical importance. The first precaution to take with any potential sexual partner is to have a conversation about personal health and previous sexual involvements. If you cannot discuss these issues with a potential partner, you are not ready to engage in intimate sexual activity with that person. One value that should shape such a conversation is *emet,* honesty. The second precaution involves the use condoms, gloves, lubricants and dental dams to minimize the risks of potentially unhealthy sexual activity. And still another is regular medical testing for anyone who is sexually active outside the context of a permanent, monogamous partnership.

When we speak of "justification" for young women providing oral sex, I am left to wonder who is responsible when behavior like this happens. There is a great opportunity for us to have conversations with young women and young men to explore these ideas thoughtfully before they become behaviors. —J.G.K.

Sexual activity should never take place where there is deception or intentional nondisclosure; where it is occurring even partly because of economic, social, emotional or physical coercion; or where there is a significant risk of injury or damage to anyone's physical or emotional health. For example, when a young woman provides oral sex to a young man outside of the context of a more mutual sexual relationship, this is often in a situation where there is subtle emotional or social coercion based upon age, gender and other factors. Issues of power, self-image and the way the recipient of such sexual favors views the person providing them often make these acts more detrimental than they appear. Given the health dangers (STDs can be transmitted in this fashion.) and coercion involved, there can be no sufficient justification for this behavior.

The mixture of sexual activity, alcohol and drugs is not commonly discussed. I think it merits conversation not only in regard to teenagers and younger adults but for everyone. The marketing of alcohol is highly eroticized in our culture. Where do we experience a counter-narrative to the one presented in the media that sex, drugs and alcohol go together? —S.P.W

Parents have a particularly significant responsibility to help their children navigate the challenges of sexuality as teenagers. Often the imposition of strict rules for teenagers — curfews, prohibitions against sexual activity, curfews at night, and severe consequences for the use of alcohol and drugs — can help provide children with a safe "out" from the pressures they experience at school and among peers. A frank and open conversation with your teenager may help you to create rules together that will support your teenager's need for protection and safety. —S.C.R.

In matters of sexual activity, a huge gap often exists between the prohibited and the ideal. Caught in that gap, individuals must sometimes make difficult choices about what they will do. One helpful way to think about these choices is to consider the status of a particular relationship, as reflected in several different measures: 1. How long and how well do you know each other? 2. What is the nature of your mutual commitment, if any? 3. How much are you physically attracted to the person? 4. What is your level of trust? 5. What are your motivations for sexual activity besides mutual attraction? 6. What are the risks to each of you? 7. What effect will sexual activity have on the relationship in the future?

Alcohol and drugs often interfere with people's ability to make careful decisions about whether to begin a sexual relationship and if so, how far to go. This is particularly the case for teenagers and younger adults. The hope that a one-night stand will develop into a meaningful, long-term relationship is generally illusory. Sexual activity for its own sake is not necessarily wrong, but potential partners need to be realistic and honest with themselves about the nature of the relationship and their hopes for it.

Sex with a friend is not casual sex. When one engages in sexual intimacy with a friend, the experience of intimacy grows out of the preexisting friendship and involves a risk that the friendship may be transformed by this new level of intimacy, for good or for ill. —L.J.E.

In a paradigm where the ideal sexual context is an emotionally intimate, mutually committed relationship, the permitted sexual activity furthest from that is anonymous, safe sex that provides physical pleasure and satisfaction but little else. As emotional connection, communication, commitment and trust grow, any sexual activity moves in the direction of the ideal. It moves closer still to that ideal when one feels genuinely understood and accepted by one's partner. When one senses transcendence and the presence of the divine in a sexual exchange, one is near the ideal.

Sex outside the context of a committed relationship often generates a wall between sexual activity and emotional intimacy. This can interfere with the power of sexual activity to create emotional intimacy with another partner at a later time. That is why many single people

choose not to engage in sex outside of a committed relationship, though others do willingly opt for casual sex
at some stages in their lives. In the absence of prospects
for finding an emotionally intimate partner, some people
adopt casual sex as the best available option. This may
be the case whether they have never been partnered or
are widowed or divorced. For them, casual sexual activity—perhaps sex with a friend—provides pleasure in the
absence of sexual activity that is closer to the ideal.

Some people choose to live together without being
married. This option does not have the same status as
kidushin (marriage, from the same Hebrew root as the
word for holy, *kadosh*). A marriage, whether sanctioned
by legal authorities or not, has the highest level of sanctity. Living together is a higher state than a more casual
sexual relationship because it involves continuity, ongoing intimacy and a commitment to shared living that often
includes a commitment to fidelity. One step up from that
is living together while engaged. In contemporary society these arrangements are often steps toward a wedding

Living with another person as a couple and building a household together itself
creates the possibility of *kidushin*. Early rabbinic law, like common law, recognized
that cohabitation with the intent of being married itself creates a marriage. —L.J.E.

Distinguishing between casual sex and living together is a wonderful revaluing of
a trend historically called "living in sin." It reminds us of the sanctity of a commitment to living together. —J.G.K.

or a commitment ceremony. Because of unfair laws and other forms of discrimination, many people in same-sex relationships do not have marriage as an option. When such people make a private commitment to a long-term covenantal relationship with each other, the community should recognize their relationship as having a high level of sanctity.

The spectrum of sexual activity—from a quick good-night kiss or a brief caress to lengthy, passionate love-making—is very broad. No matter how much a person is willing to do sexually, in any given situation every person has limits. Going beyond those limits would, at the least, make that person uncomfortable. People should not be pushed into doing things for which they are not ready or about which they feel uncomfortable with a particular person in a particular time and place.

Demands by one partner on the other regarding how that partner dresses, acts in public, or looks at or interacts with others are often actually expressions of a desire to control one's partner. Such demands are often associated with family violence and abuse, and they should be seen as warning signs in any relationship. —S.C.R.

Similarly, people have very different ideas about the appropriateness of public displays of affection. Part of that is concern about what may make others uncomfortable, and part is modesty, *tz'ni'ut*. *Tz'ni'ut* as a virtue is much valued in rabbinic Judaism, but when modesty is translated into behavioral norms and imposed on others, the result is not necessarily so positive. Exaggerated demands for *tz'ni'ut* can be both overly repressive and regressive, and they have often been used to reinforce the historically second-class social position of women. Demands for *tz'ni'ut* are often viewed with suspicion, but it is also true that *tz'ni'ut* has several positive functions. A modest person understands that very personal things should be kept private and that certain ways of dressing and talking can attract unwanted attention. If one develops the virtue of *tz'ni'ut* within oneself, then, instead of the repressive external imposition of others' judgments about how modesty should be reflected in personal behavior, one can make one's own decisions wisely.

Tz'ni'ut, like any other form of personal social behavior, is not merely a personal choice. It reflects social values, cultural traditions and shared communal attitudes. In a culture that highly prizes individual autonomy, we often find it hard to accept external norms, but social interaction requires shared values and expectations. The way we choose to present ourselves is a statement. How others respond to us creates a conversation. One hopes that this conversation reflects openness and respect for all its participants. —L.J.E.

Many elderly people retain interest in sexual activity. It is important for personnel at care facilities serving this population to respect the right of elderly people to privacy and self-determination in this area. The adult children of elders also need to treat this area of their parents' lives with respect, without making assumptions in any direction. People with disabilities also deserve the opportunity to shape their own sex lives. Where possible, open, non-judgmental conversation will benefit all concerned.

Sexual activity within freely chosen limits with the right person at a good time and place is delightful. It not only provides the opportunity to give and receive physical pleasure; it strengthens interpersonal connection and brings deep joy.

Gay, Lesbian, and Bisexual People and their Relationships

Attitudes toward gay relationships have become much more accepting in recent years. The presumption of a patriarchal society that depends upon having many children for prosperity and for raising large, successful armies is that heterosexuality will not simply be much more common; it will be the norm, as suggested above. In our time, there is good reason not to maximize the birthrate, and new reproductive technologies and effective contraception

Patriarchal cultures are not necessarily opposed to homosexual acts and behaviors. In the classical world, where a high level of childbirth balanced the high death rate, fathering children and bearing children were social duties. Homosexual relations did not preclude a man or a woman from fulfilling their procreative duties to family, community and society. In certain patriarchal cultures, specific forms of sexual activity between males were seen as helpful in fostering male bonding and providing an appropriate way to channel male sexual desires. The greatest challenge to social stability was not homosexuality or premarital sex, but adultery. —L.J.E.

It is accurate to say that there has always been homosexual sex. The terms gay, lesbian and bisexual are social constructions that go beyond the sexual act into realms of socio-political discourse. —N.H.M.

In recent decades, volumes have been written about the prohibition in Leviticus (18:22 and 20:13), "Do not lie with a male the lyings of a woman," and about what it might mean for Jews and gay people today. These verses are found within the section of the Torah known as the Holiness Code. The essence of the Holiness Code is summed up by Hillel in his famous statement of the Torah on one foot: "That which is hateful to you, do not do to your neighbor." A queer-positive reading begins here. Since the Holiness Code is about justice, and often about protecting those with less power against abuse by those with greater power, then a restatement of the prohibition for our contemporary social context might be something like: "Do not use your sexual power as a destructive force against another person, to denigrate, humiliate, dominate or harm them." When we get fixated on reading the verse as a prohibition against same-sex desire, we can miss out on receiving real Torah about what it means to live into holiness. —D.N./T.K.

have to a considerable extent decoupled procreation and sexual activity. Major economic and social changes that have minimized gender-role differences in postindustrial society have helped us to substantially reduce patriarchy in North America and elsewhere. In an increasingly egalitarian world that is more fluid regarding gender roles, the structural impediments to non-heterosexual relationships have largely been removed.

The talmudic rabbis' understanding that the Torah prohibits all male homosexual acts stems from the fact that those acts were viewed as the perverted acts of heterosexual men. Some recent scholarship suggests that the biblical use of the term *to'eva* (abomination) may refer to a cultic violation, in this case involving the imitation of the fertility rituals of some non-Israelite cults. Contemporary understandings of homosexuality recognize that it is not about heterosexuals doing something outside the natural

I have heard Rabbi Steven Greenberg present a complex and impressive analysis of commentaries on the Leviticus prohibition of "a man lying with a man as with a woman" to indicate that the true prohibition is against any abusive sex. —S.P.W.

Two narratives in the Hebrew Bible that deal with the behavior prohibited in the verses in Leviticus are found in Genesis 19 and Judges 19. These are parallel narratives in which traveling strangers are offered hospitality by a local resident, and the townsfolk demand that the travelers be turned over to a mob to be raped. The rape is clearly not an act of sexual intimacy but rather a demonstration of the mob's power and authority over a stranger through an act of dominance and humiliation. As modern readers, we find these stories horrifying, but within the context of ancient Near Eastern literature, Leviticus 18:22 and 20:13 should be understood as prohibitions against the abuse of power through sexual penetration – the power of a mob over a visiting stranger or the power of a stronger man over a weaker one. —D.N./T.K.

Perhaps not regulating lesbian sexual activity in a patriarchal society reflects the view in that world that a sexual act was defined by the presence of a penis. —J.G.K.

order of things, but about people who are genuinely attracted to people of the same sex fulfilling their natural
needs and desires. This scientific realization—that there
have always been gay men, lesbians and bisexuals even
when they were not publicly accepted—ends the notion
that male homosexual acts are a *to'eva,* as the rabbis understood the Torah (see Leviticus 18:22). Lesbian sexual
activity was never designated as an abomination, perhaps
because there was no *hashhatat zera,* or perhaps because
in a patriarchal society, the only female sexual activity men felt the need to regulate was activity leading to
pregnancy.

Though same-sex couples should, as a civil right, be allowed to marry, it would be
a mistake to assume that all committed same-sex couples would opt for the heterosexual marriage model if it were legal and available to everyone. In the view of
some, the structure of same-sex relationships plays out in unique ways. —N.H.M.

All people have an obligation not to inflict their bigotry on others, but the case of
one minority group expressing bigotry toward another is also sadly ironic. —J.G.K.

Same-sex attraction and opposite-sex attraction are not polar opposites. Many current understandings see them as part of the spectrum of sexuality, with people toward the middle of the spectrum attracted to both sexes (bisexual). If a rigid patriarchal order were needed or if maximizing procreation were important to society's future, there might be a reason to insist that people conform to heterosexual norms. But given that donor insemination, surrogacy and adoption are options and that increasing numbers of single people and gay couples raise children, all forms of attraction, regardless of gender, can and should be regarded as equally legitimate, and gay relationships and sexual activity should be analyzed in the same way that straight ones are. The values relevant to decisions about heterosexual relationships apply equally well to homosexual ones. Of course, gay men and lesbians have access to the same sanctity and are subject to the same limitations, such as proscriptions against violence, incest, exploitation, pedophilia and pederasty.

Gay culture often developed under conditions of violent repression. Gay men experienced great difficulty in having openly gay relationships within most mainstream Western cultures, including traditional Judaism. Perhaps that partly explains the historical role of anonymous sexual encounters within gay culture. With the rapidly growing acceptance of same-sex marriages, committed gay relationships are developing in greater numbers, even as society's growing comfort with the sexual expression characteristic of gay culture is having a positive influence.

Many people are not comfortable with gay, lesbian and bisexual people because of their discomfort with their own sexual identities. Such people have an obligation not to inflict their discomfort and bigotry on others. The suicide rate among gay and lesbian young people is high in part because of the prejudice and oppression they encounter. Those who overtly or covertly oppress or harass gay and lesbian young people or adults are behaving unethically.

Monogamy

For the last millennium Ashkenazi Jews have seen monogamous marriage as the primary locus for sexual activity. While divorce has always existed within the Jewish community, it has been relatively infrequent. However, in recent years changing financial and social circumstances have led to increased rates of divorce and remarriage—a shift from monogamy to serial monogamy. Monogamous marriage has remained a dominant social form because at best it provides emotional intimacy, companionship, stability for raising children and a relatively efficient economic unit, while avoiding the complexity and jealousy that can plague other sexual arrangements. Monogamy has long been the dominant social form in Christian

Monogamy—a committed, lifelong, binary relationship between adults—is a basic metaphor in Jewish life. Mystically, the intimate joining of a loving couple expresses the covenant between God and Israel, the bond between the Creator and creation, and the possibility of moving beyond this world of separation to the world of unity. Mythically, humanity was created as a couple, emerging at the same time and bound together as one flesh. The intimate bond between a committed couple recreates this sense of primal unity and equality. —L.J.E.

The biblical metaphor of God as husband and the people Israel as wife creates both unique opportunities and immense challenges for us today. On the one hand, the marriage metaphor conveys a relationship of intimacy and commitment between God and the community. On the other hand, it reinforces patriarchal models of marriage wherein only the female partner is bound to absolute fidelity and where any disruption in the relationship is blamed on her. —T.K.

societies, and Jews tend to conform to such external structures when they are not in tension with Jewish values and practice. The sanctity of monogamous marriage (*kidushin*) has long been appreciated in the Jewish community.

The ideal of monogamy is expressed in Genesis 2:24: "Hence a man leaves his father and mother and clings to his wife." —L.K.

It is important to remember that in biblical times, a man involved in a sexual relationship with a married woman faced social condemnation (Proverbs 5:20-23; 6:29) and serious legal consequences (Deuteronomy 22:22). Rabbinic teachings concerning sexual behavior focused for the most part on controlling men's sexual behavior. —L.J.E.

Adultery

Adultery involves having a sexual relationship with some-one other than one's spouse during a marriage. In biblical times, adultery was defined as a married woman having a sexual relationship with a man other than her husband. It was irrelevant whether the man involved was married or not. This is the form of adultery that is forbidden in the Ten Commandments. Adultery violates the covenant of marriage, which involves a promise and commitment to fidelity. This biblical definition reflects a double stan-dard, in which men's and women's sexual activities are judged differently. From the perspective of egalitarian values, this double standard is unacceptable, and it has gradually been disappearing since the sexual revolution of the 1960s. It is now broadly understood that the com-mitment to fidelity is equally binding on men and wom-en, and contemporary *ketubot* (marriage contracts) and wedding vows reflect that reality.

Adultery is wrong. It violates the basic understanding of a marriage or committed relationship. The desire of one partner in a relationship to enter into an intimate relationship with another person indicates that there is something dysfunctional within the marriage. The willingness of one partner to ignore the breach of com-mitment by the other partner does not make it right. The offense against the rela-tionship, however, is not the cause of the dysfunction. Healing the relationship or dissolving it in a healthy manner requires not only *teshuva*/repentance, and *seliha*/forgiveness, but also *heshbon hanefesh*/deep searching into the hearts of the partners and the nature of their relationship. —L.J.E.

When marriage vows or commitment ceremony vows are broken and this becomes known, it creates deep pain and a breakdown in trust. Infidelity may also introduce health risks from STDs into the marriage. Many marriages are able to recover from infidelity through a lengthy and challenging period of rebuilding trust, but that is not always possible.

Some couples agree to suspend the part of their marriage vows that deal with fidelity. That may occur when one partner becomes uninterested in sex or has a physical disability that prevents such activity. While that kind of decision obviously poses risks to a marriage, those risks may be lower than the risks of any of the other alternatives available to the couple.

A situation may arise where one partner is completely incapacitated. For example, a partner with advanced Alzheimer's disease and no remaining cognitive abilities may be institutionalized. In such a situation, the healthy partner is still married and is responsible for tending to the impaired partner's needs, but for all intents and purposes, the healthy partner is living alone. While still legally married, such a partner can build a life that allows for intimacy with others, since the impaired partner can

---

I want to underscore the importance of exploring the issue of sexual relations in the case of a partner's dementia far in advance, while the partners are still of sound mind. People do not become "cured" from Alzheimer's disease and they cannot speak about what it was like for them to experience Alzheimer's-associated dementia, so we do not know the extent to which their partners' sexual behavior may be stressful or distressing. The person with dementia may sometimes be more aware than we realize. —J.G.K.

no longer meet those needs. As long as the healthy partner cares for the ailing spouse, the healthy partner can develop a sexual relationship with someone else without violating marriage vows, for under these conditions this does not significantly harm the institutionalized partner. These potential issues should be explored while partners are healthy, as part of a discussion of medical preferences in case of serious illness (see the "Bioethics" section of *A Guide to Jewish Practice*). Such arrangements might be part of an explicit agreement between the partners as they consider the possibility of developing dementia. When such arrangements are put into effect, they can affect other familial relationships. Where possible, the healthy parent should discuss the situation with the couple's children.

The real question here is whether the marriage relationship is intact when one partner cannot, for reasons beyond his or her control, fulfill the mutual commitments of the marriage. In the case of advanced dementia, it seems that the circumstances mitigate the objective breach. Specific situations such as this, in which the well-being of the impaired partner depends upon the well-being of the caregiver, require a high level of honesty and openness. I would suggest seeking guidance and counsel from a skilled therapist and the counsel of a sensitive and knowledgeable rabbi or other spiritual teacher. At best, we are left with a painful response to a painful situation.   —L.J.E.

For more than 40 years, I have worked with very old people, aged 80 to 101, who have been diagnosed with Alzheimer's dementia. I have found that they have an intuitive knowing that defies cognition. A 90-year-old nursing-home resident who had undressed in public smiled as she explained to me, "It's better when you're crazy. Then it doesn't matter what you do." When sensory cells no longer tell the brain where the body is and social controls vanish, human needs remain. The need for respect, identity and nurturing persist, though present-day reality becomes blurred. The old person diagnosed with a dementia is aware. Those making choices about what to do in the presence of such elders need to take this into account. —Naomi Feil, executive director, Validation Training Institute, Cleveland, Ohio

Jewish Polygamy and Monogamy—
A Complex History

The Torah includes accounts of polygamy—think of
Jacob, Rachel and Leah—as well as relationships with
concubines, such as Zilpa and Bilha, who bore some of
Jacob's children. Of course in the biblical account, such
arrangements consisted of one man with multiple wom-
en. This reflects not only the demands of patriarchy, but
also the difficulty in that time for a woman attempting
to live alone. Larger family units were more efficient
and safer. The tradition of polygyny — being married to
more than one wife at a time — has continued to the
present day among Sephardim (descendants of Spanish
Jewry) and Jews of Eastern countries such as Yemen,
though only a minority of Sephardic men have ever had
more than one wife. The number of Jewish polygamous

It is noteworthy that the biblical Hebrew word for co-wife is *tzara*/trouble. In
the postbiblical Jewish experience, polygamy, although often permitted, has been
rare for many of the same reasons. At the beginning of the 11th century, Rabbenu
Gershom ben Judah, *M'or Hagola,* instituted a number of significant reforms for
European (Ashkenazi) Jewry that offered additional protection to women. These
reforms included the prohibition of polygamy and the requirement for mutual consent in the case of divorce. Even among the Jews of Muslim lands where the pre-
vailing social customs allowed for polygamous households, such arrangements were
uncommon. —L.J.E.

The Torah describes the relationship between the two wives of Elkana with the
word *tzara* (I Samuel 1:6), which means "misfortune, affliction, trouble, distress."
Does polygamy carry a greater likelihood of these? —L.K.

Although polygamy is common in the stories of the Patriarchs, the Torah's writers
seem to need to find a justification to explain it: Sarah wanted Abraham to have a
child by Hagar; Jacob had to marry two women because of his father-in-law's deception. —(L.K.)

families has shrunk in recent years because the practice has been banned in the State of Israel, though men who immigrated to Israel with multiple wives were allowed to stay married to them. Today, with most paid work involving an employer outside the family, a much larger family unit does not automatically have an economic advantage. Ashkenazi Jews (those of German and East European descent) have officially observed the ban on polygamy declared by the halakhic authority of Mayence, Rabbenu Gershom, in the eleventh century.

Scholars of Jewish sexual ethics in America have overwhelmingly supported monogamy as the highest form of marriage. Clearly, egalitarian values require either that men be allowed only one wife or that women be allowed more than one husband. Since polygamy is against the law in all North American states and provinces, and since Jews follow the dictum of *dina d'malkhuta dina*, the law of the land is the law, monogamy is naturally the pattern of practice in the North American Jewish community. Furthermore, those who are known for practicing polygamy in violation of the law in North America are described as patriarchal, and underage women are often

Open marriage and polygamy are never acceptable. The goal of Jewish ethical teaching is not merely to establish honest and functional interpersonal relationships, but also to guide people into living a lifestyle that reifies and manifests the unfolding Jewish understanding of God as present in their lives. *Kashrut,* the system of Jewish dietary laws, provides an analogy. While it is obviously forbidden to eat poisonous food, most nonkosher food is wholesome and nourishing. Following a kosher diet or a vegetarian diet expresses a set of values beyond the commitment to eating good food. Prior to deciding whether to eat pork, a Jew should explore whether *kashrut* as it has developed and/or as it is currently practiced best represents the spiritual values we hope to express through our pattern of eating. Our relationships should reflect our spiritual values. —L.J.E.

involved. All of this creates an unsavory reputation for polygamy. But what if the law and the practitioners were different? It is not obvious that monogamy is automatically a morally higher form of relationship than polygamy. If those involved reached an explicit agreement in favor of some version of egalitarian polygamy or open marriage, there would be no violation of integrity or of a covenant or a contractual agreement. Would it be acceptable under those conditions?

Maintaining intimacy and trust requires good communication and the effective management of jealousy. This is difficult enough to achieve between two people. It is considerably more difficult among three or more, considering the relationships between all the dyads as well as among the group as a whole. The difficulty of managing trust and communication and of avoiding jealousy is well illustrated in the biblical stories of Abraham, Sarah and Hagar, and of Jacob, Rachel, Leah, Bilha, and Zilpa and their children. But the fact that something may be difficult to do well does not necessarily mean that it ought to be forbidden. Perhaps some people can manage it successfully and live enriched lives as a result.

Open Marriage and Polyamory

The traditional form of the Jewish wedding explicitly commits the woman — but not the man — to sexual fidelity. She is *mekudeshet*, set aside, for him, but the reverse is not true. Egalitarian versions of the wedding vows and the *ketuba* (written marriage contract) imply that both husband and wife are committed to marital fidelity. The other egalitarian solution to the inequality in the traditional marriage agreement would be to require fidelity of neither partner. Polyamory allows for multiple romantic and sexual relationships that are not concealed from other lovers. While this does not solve the problems that can characterize polygamy—jealousy and challenges to communication, trust and intimacy—it does not necessarily violate secular law. And since both parties freely enter such an arrangement and both parties have the power to end it, polyamory avoids some possible forms of exploitation. Adultery generally involves the violation of vows and the need for secrecy. Polyamory, which does not have such difficulties, is preferable from that perspective, as

Many stories about early life on Israel's socialistic kibbutzim indicate that polyamory was the acceptable norm among kibbutzniks at that time. The fact that this is no longer the moral norm in Israeli society suggests the inherent difficulty in maintaining long-term, loving relationships without the help of fidelity. —S.C.R.

It is important to distinguish between polyamory in general and long-term, committed romantic relationships that permit sexual activity outside the relationship, generally with certain rules about what activities are permitted and with whom. I have come to know many people who take this style of relationship very seriously and who describe it in covenantal language. Partners in such relationships are both deeply committed to one another, but they do not expect to have all of their sexual needs met within the relationship. —J.G.K.

well. Clearly, successful polyamory would require considerable maturity, communication that relieves jealousy, and a high level of flexibility.

One caution that should be considered regarding both polygamy and polyamory is that romantic and sexual relationships need to be viewed against the background of the implications for others. Do children get less or more attention from polyamorous or polygamous parents? Are children raised with equal care? What about the needs and interests of aging parents and other family members? One of the moral considerations regarding romantic and sexual relationships is their impact on the family. Another is their impact on the community. If polyamory were to be broadly practiced, would this destabilize the community? The common reaction of people who have grown up with monogamy as the only accepted social form is to assume that polyandry and polygyny, if not exploitative, would surely be destabilizing. But evidence from practices elsewhere in the world does not justify this reaction.

While considering open marriage and polyamory might be interesting in terms of an abstract philosophical discussion, engaging in such relationships is ill-conceived and ill-advised from the perspective of practical ethics. Good ethical practice directs us not to enter relationships that are prone to difficulty. While one might be able to argue that such relationships are workable, the ethical person seeks simplicity, honesty and transparency in all areas of his or her life. Polygamy, polyandry and polyamory are not viable options. —L.J.E.

Jewish tradition and practice offer no precedent for polyamory. Can a version of its practice be compatible with such Jewish values as *tz'ni'ut*, modesty? While pockets of polyamory do exist in the United States, its practice is not broadly socially acceptable. A small amount of literature exists about it, but there has not been sufficient documented experience with it to indicate its strengths and weaknesses as a social form. Such experience would allow for a more thorough moral position on it to be taken. While private, small-scale experiments with polyamory have taken place, its future as a moral option is uncertain.

Sexual relations with three or more partners or multiple couples in the same space have occurred in many different times and places. Even assuming that the adults are consenting, this raises several issues. While it can add a new level of excitement to a relationship, it can also destabilize it. Having multiple partners carries an enhanced possibility of exposure to STDs. In addition, obvious questions of privacy and modesty arise. Do the potential pleasures of such activities outweigh the problems and risks? Jewish tradition has generally said no.

Prostitution

Prostitution has existed in most societies from earliest times. Jews have visited prostitutes, and Jews have become prostitutes. In our time, prostitution is often entangled with organized crime, drugs, trafficking in slavery, violence and other forms of exploitation. Engaging in prostitution in most places is wrong because it violates the principle of *dina d'malkhuta dina* and because it is associated with other major moral problems and risks.

But what about prostitution where it is legal, regulated and reasonably well compensated? What if some people prefer working as prostitutes to working for low wages and long hours under exploitative conditions? One objection to prostitution is that it turns sexual activity into a commodity, and is thus degrading to the prostitute in particular and to women in general, since the vast majority of prostitutes are women. Some people marry

Prostitution is wrong. The pursuit of pleasure is not a Jewish spiritual and ethical goal. The commercialization of sex, including but not limited to prostitution, objectifies sexual relations and the participants in the relations. It treats people as objects, and turns our most intimate form of self-expression into a mere activity. Since a vision of sexual relations as sacred intimacy is not universally accepted and not always attainable, a demand exists for other forms of sexual expression, and a market exists to meet that demand. To be healthy and function well, societies need to regulate behaviors and protect their members. There is a difference, however, between what is permissible and what is ethically and spiritually life enhancing. Legalizing prostitution, protecting sex workers and regulating the distribution of pornography may be proper activities for a government. However, they are not the best expression of ethical values. —L.J.E.

for money. Others have sex with their partners to keep peace in the family. We do not always have sex because we feel like making love. In a perfect world, everyone would find sexual satisfaction with others who have the same goals, and no one would be driven to prostitution because of economic need. Some argue that all prostitution is exploitative and therefore immoral. Those who disagree should at the least limit frequenting prostitutes to those places where prostitutes and those who engage them are physically, economically and legally protected.

Even under those conditions, prostitution can violate marriage vows. A married person who has a sexual relationship with a prostitute is an adulterer. Such activity may pose less of a threat to the marriage than an illicit romantic relationship, but no breach of the commitment to fidelity can be viewed lightly.

We should also be concerned about the potential negative impact of the prostitute on the client and of engaging in objectification. —J.G.K.

Gender Identity

Western society classifies people as either male or female. Most of Western society understands gender and sex to be binary, though sex is physical, and gender is socially constructed. However, gender and sex have been understood differently in different times and different places, and sexual identity has proved to be far more variegated

Some of the gender variations discussed in the Talmud are *androgynos, tumtum, saris ḥama, saris adam* and *aylonit*. In Mishna Bikkurim 4.1-5, the text describes the ways that an *androgynos* should in some ways be treated legally like a man, in some ways like a woman, in some ways like both a man and a woman, and in some ways like neither a man nor a woman. The section concludes with the minority opinion of Rabbi Yose, who says, "The *androgynos* is *bri'a bifnei atzma,* a created being of its own, and the sages could not decide if he was a man or a woman. But this is not the case for the *tumtum*—sometimes a *tumtum* is a man, and sometimes a *tumtum* is a woman."

The entire chapter is remarkable for its interest in how Torah law, which addresses only male and female genders, should be applied to people whose gender isn't easily described by those two categories. Rabbi Yose's opinion is even more astonishing. He seems to abandon the majority's strategy of trying to understand an *androgynos* through the binary gender categories of "man" and "woman," and instead proposes a new category: *br'ia bifnei atzma,* a created being of its own kind.

This is only one of hundreds of rabbinic texts that deal with *androgynos, tumtum* and other ways of describing human genders. The texts are diverse and fascinating. So far there is no scholarly consensus about what these texts may have meant to the people who first transmitted them. But for us, these rabbinic texts have become fertile soil for a growing literature of liberation.   —D.N.

Cutting-edge issues such as those evoked by discussions of transsexuality and gender identity reflect exactly what we mean by Judaism as an evolving religious civilization. These issues require us to demand of ourselves and our community a flexibility in ethical decision making that reflects both contemporary scientific research and openness to continued moral dialogue and examination of prejudices from our past.   —S.C.R.

than previously thought. The Talmud recognizes many different kinds of gender statuses other than male and female, several of them involving different kinds of genitalia. In contemporary North America, about one in 2,000 babies is born with genitalia that are not simply male or female. These babies are described as "intersex." Intersexual infants sometimes undergo surgery very early, at an age much too young to obtain their consent, in an attempt to make them male or female.

The Intersex Society of North America condemns genital surgeries on infants and young children that are responses to parental distress, not to a problem experienced by the child. — J.G.K.

"Intersex" is one way that people with atypical sex describe their sex. In the medical world, the term "disorders of sex development" or "DSD" is increasingly being used to describe the constellation of genetic, hormonal, developmental and physical characteristics that make some people's bodies difficult to characterize using the categories of "male" and "female." Some advocates use the words "differences of sex development" in place of "disorders of sex development" when unpacking the acronym "DSD." The American Academy of Pediatrics adopted a "Consensus Agreement" in 2006 to suggest medical protocols for children born with DSDs. The protocols call for an interdisciplinary team (including a social worker and a psychologist), and maximum family education, involvement and empowerment. They recommend that babies born with atypical sex characteristics be assigned a gender of either male or female early on, but that any surgeries that are not medically necessary be delayed until these children become old enough to develop their own gender identity and to participate in making decisions about their bodies. — D.N.

Rabbis and Jewish communities can play a critical role in welcoming babies, children and adults with atypical sex characteristics and their families. We can draw on our sacred texts to affirm the holiness of the full range of sexual and gender identities as a reflection of God's wondrously diverse creation. We can educate ourselves and our communities about sex differences and about the experiences of people with atypical sex. We can look at our assumptions about gender and sex, and we can have open, affirming communal conversations about sex and gender diversity. —D.N.

Some people, whether they are intersexual or not, perceive themselves as not fitting into the gender into which they were assigned at birth. They identify as "transgender," an umbrella term referring to all people whose inner sense of self does not match their outer physical sex. Transgender individuals are people who were born female but consider themselves male, those who were born male but consider themselves female, and those whose identity falls between the genders. Just as the Talmud was able to recognize many different kinds of gender statuses, people who perceive themselves as misclassified by birth or surgery or who see themselves as intersexual should be encouraged to find their own way regarding their gender

Today, transphobia, the fear of gender variance in society, impacts all parts of life. Children who do not gender-conform are often met with physical, verbal and sexual cruelty and are sometimes forced to drop out of school. In some cases, families eventually disown such children and deprive them of their economic support systems. Transgender adults face significant obstacles to accessing employment, healthcare, police protection and other essential services. Throughout the world each year, more than 100 transgender people are murdered in gender-based crimes. These injustices can be traced to the idea that there can and should be only two types of human beings – male and female.

From before we are born, people ask, "Is it a boy or a girl?" From the moment of birth onward most facets of our lives – the clothes we are told to wear, the activities we are anticipated to like, the careers and hobbies we are encouraged to pursue, the loving relationships we are expected to have – are guided by the answer to this crucial question. The past few decades of feminist organizing have deeply questioned whether we can (or should) see gender as an essential way to divide up humanity. And yet most of us 21st-century people were still raised to believe that whether we are a girl or a boy is a simple, unchangeable fact.

Rabbinic texts speak in a different voice. The Mishna, Talmud and Jewish law codes are filled with references to genders beyond male and female. All these genders appear frequently in classical Jewish texts – the *tumtum* appears 119 times in the Babylonian Talmud alone! And yet gender diversity is seldom discussed as an integral part of Jewish sacred texts or as a spiritual resource of our tradition. Genders

identity. Those who discriminate by word or deed against transgender, intersexual or gender-nonconforming individuals are acting in an unethical way.

Given that gender roles are no longer as relevant to one's professional, partnering or social statuses, the distinction between genders does not have the significance it once had. Transgender individuals whose gender identity differs from the gender assigned to them by others have certain choices. They may avail themselves of hormone therapy; they may wear clothing that conforms to their inner gender identity; or they may choose to undergo sex reassignment surgery. As long as the choices they make are not medically high risk, they have the same right that all people have to find a way of representing themselves that is true to their self-understanding.

Our analysis of gender identity stems from relatively recent research, and our grasp of it can be expected to continue evolving and becoming more sophisticated. As that occurs, our use of terminology and our moral analysis of the issue will in all likelihood continue to shift as well.

that lie in between male and female are usually not afforded all of the privileges offered to men, and sometimes kept apart from the protections bestowed on women in traditional Jewish law; however, the presence of these individuals conveys a powerful and radical message to modern transgender and gender non-conforming Jews: Our existence is recognized; we are present within the most sacred texts of Jewish tradition.   —E.K.

The Jewish world still needs a great deal of education on issues of transgender if we are to avoid conditioned behaviors that are indeed hurtful and unethical. I agree that this is a new and fluid era in regard to gender identities.   —S.P.W.

What is "unsafe medically" requires a subjective evaluation and should be weighed against the emotional risk of living in a body in which you feel you do not belong.   —J.G.K.

Conclusion

This section of *A Guide to Jewish Practice* is much more powerfully subject to social and technological change than much of the rest of the guide. Utilizing the sources of Jewish tradition to adapt to the unfolding social and technological situation is a task that is never complete. As our culture evolves, family structures, gender roles, and sexual practices will inevitably evolve as well. Given the importance of these evolving elements in forming human society and shaping individual lives, it is critical that our evolving choices continue to be informed by Jewish values.

For Further Reading

The subjects of family and sexual ethics have attracted considerable scholarly and popular attention both inside and beyond the Jewish community. A plethora of available materials exists, and new books and articles come out in a steady stream, with fresh sociological and anthropological insights and technological and scientific advances. Even more than on most subjects, the literature on sexual and family ethics usually reflects strong ideological biases.

For a modern Orthodox perspective, *The Jewish Way in Love & Marriage* by Maurice Lamm (Harper & Row, 1980) is a clearly written and thorough book; its title reflects its perspective. Elliot Dorff's *Love Your Neighbor and Yourself: A Jewish Approach to Modern Personal Ethics* (Jewish Publication Society, 2003) provides an excellent Conservative perspective, as does an older volume by David Feldman, *Birth Control in Jewish Law* (New York University Press, 1968). While, like Feldman's book, not completely current on issues such as STDs, one classical Reform text of continuing importance is Eugene Borowitz's *Choosing a Sex Ethic: A Jewish Inquiry* (Schocken, 1969). Reconstructionist perspectives can be found in many articles, such as David Teutsch's, "Towards a Jewish Sex Ethic" in *Reconstructionism Today* (11.2, pp. 1, 4-7) and *The Report of the Reconstructionist Commission on Homosexuality*.

A good history of sexuality can be found in Paul Root Wolpe and Janell Carroll's *Sexuality and Gender in Society* (HarperCollins, 1996). Numerous other works also exist in this field.

For gay, lesbian, bisexual and queer perspectives, many choices exist, including *The Passionate Torah: Sex and*

Judaism (New York University Press, 2009) edited by Danya Ruttenberg; *Like Bread on the Seder Plate: Jewish Lesbians and the Transformation of Tradition* (Columbia University Press, 1998) by Rebecca Alpert; *Twice Blessed: On Being Lesbian or Gay and Jewish* (Beacon Books, 1989) edited by Christie Balka and Andy Rose; and *Queer Jews* (Routledge, 2002), edited by David Shneer and Caryn Aviv. On transgender issues, see *Balancing on the Mechitza: Transgender in Jewish Community* (North Atlantic Books, 2010), edited by Noach Dzmura.

For traditional Jewish sources, see *Sex Ethics in the Writings of Moses Maimonides* by Fred Rosner and *The Holy Letter/ Iggeret Hakodesh: A Study in Jewish Sexual Morality* (Jason Aronson, 1993) edited by Seymour J. Cohen. For an understanding of the diversity of premodern Jewish sexual practice, see "Sexual Behavior in Medieval Hispano-Jewish Society" by Yom Tov Assis in *Jewish History: Essays in Honor of Chimen Abramsky* (Peter Halban Publishers Ltd., 1989), edited by Ada Rapoport-Albert and Stephen J. Zipperstein.

For secular perspectives, see *The Myth of Monogamy: Fidelity and Infidelity in Animals and People* (W.H. Freeman and Co., 2001) by David P. Barash and Judith Eve Lipton, M.D., *Polyamory: The New Love without Limits: Secrets of Sustainable Intimate Relations* (IntiNet Resource Center, 1997) *by Deborah M. Anapol*; and *Touching our Strength: The Erotic as Power and the Love of God* (4Shadows Books, 1989), edited by Carter Heyward.

Biographies of Contributors

Lewis John Eron, Ph.D., a graduate of the Reconstructionist Rabbinical College, is the Jewish Community Chaplain for the Jewish Federation of Southern New Jersey in Cherry Hill, NJ, and Director of Religious Services at the Lions Gate Continuing Care Retirement Community in Voorhees, NJ.

Rabbi Richard Hirsh is Executive Director of the Reconstructionist Rabbinical Association, a past Editor of *The Reconstructionist,* and a former congregational rabbi. He teaches at the Reconstructionist Rabbinical College.

Leah Kamionkowski is a certified public accountant. A vice president of the Jewish Reconstructionist Federation, she is a member of Kol HaLev in Cleveland, OH.

Tamar Kamionkowski, Ph.D. is the Vice President for Academic Affairs and Associate Professor of Biblical Civilization at the Reconstructionist Rabbinical College.

Rabbi Jason Gary Klein is a 2002 graduate of RRC. He has served on the boards of the RRA and RRC and is a faculty member at Camp JRF. He currently serves as director of Hillel at UMBC (University of Maryland, Baltimore County).

Rabbi Elliot Kukla is a rabbi at the Bay Area Healing Center in San Francisco. Elliot was ordained by Hebrew Union College in Los Angles and trained in chaplaincy at the University of California at San Francisco (UCSF) Medical Center Langley Porter Psychiatric Institute. His articles on gender and Judaism are published and anthologized widely; he has lectured on Jewish perspectives on stigma and diversity across the country.

Rabbi Nina H. Mandel serves Congregation Beth El in Sunbury, PA. She is also a lecturer in the Department of Philosophy and Religion at Susquehanna University.

Rabbi Devra Noily (RRC 2009) has been active in queer Jewish communities for twenty years, and has served congregations Sha'ar Zahav in San Francisco, Beit HaChidush in Amsterdam and Bet Haverim in Atlanta, GA. Dev is currently the Director of the Kehilla Community Synagogue School in Piedmont, CA.

Rabbi Barbara Penzner serves Temple Hillel B'nai Torah in West Roxbury, MA. A past president of the Reconstructionist Rabbinical Association, she has lived in Israel for two years as a Jerusalem Fellow and worked as a consultant to the Combined Jewish Philanthropies of Boston.

Rabbi Steven Carr Reuben is senior rabbi of Kehillat Israel Reconstructionist Synagogue in Pacific Palisades, CA. He is the author of five books on raising ethical children and on aspects of intermarriage, as well as many articles.

Rabbi David A. Teutsch is the Wiener Professor of Contemporary Jewish Civilization and Director of the Levin-Lieber Program in Jewish Ethics at the Reconstructionist Rabbinical College. A past president of the College, he was Editor-in-Chief of the *Kol Haneshamah* prayerbook series.

Rabbi Sheila Peltz Weinberg is Outreach Director and a staff member teaching meditation at the Institute for Jewish Spirituality. She has previously served as a congregational rabbi, Hillel director and community relations professional.

Index

Polygyny 66, 70
Potiphar's wife 15
Premarital sex 56
Prohibited sexual partners 44-46
Prostitution 15, 72-73
Proverbs 19, 22, 25, 62
P'ru ur'yu 17, 39

Queer 3, 5, 19, 56

Rabbenu Gershom ben Judah 66-67
Rabbi Yose 74
Rachel 12, 66, 68
Ramban 43
Rape 12, 15, 46, 57
Rebbe Nachman 32
Rebecca 12
Religious consistency 36
Ruth 19, 38

Safe sex 42, 51
Same-sex relationships 53, 56-60
Sarah 6, 66, 68
Seliha 63
Separation 17, 33-35
Sephardim 66
Serial monogamy 61
Sex and the elderly 55
Sexual abuse 33
Sexual activity 3, 15, 39-44, 47-55, 57, 59, 69, 72
Sexual coercion 40, 43, 45-46, 49
Sexual ethics 3-4, 67
Sexual identity 3, 74
Sexual intercourse 41-42
Sexual pleasure 41-43
Sexuality 3-4, 39-40, 49, 56-57, 59, 74

Sexually transmitted diseases (STDs) 42, 48-49, 64, 71
Shalom 41
Shekhina 11
Sh'ma 23
Sh'lom bayit 13-14, 28, 33, 47
Sh'mirat haguf 48
Sperm donor 30
Stepfamilies 16, 29, 45
Surrogate parent 30

Talmud 11, 17, 20-21, 25-26, 33, 41, 57, 74-76
Tamar 15
Tanakh 18
Ten Commandments 26, 63
Torah 12, 17, 20, 23, 25-26, 41, 55-58, 66, 74
Transgender 76-77
Transphobia 76
Transsexuality 3, 74
Tumtum 74, 76
Tzara 66
Tzedeka 41
Tzelem Elohim 5, 46-47
Tzimtzum 21
Tz'ni'ut 54, 71

V'ahavta 23

Yehoshua ben Perahya 16
Yir'a 25, 28
Yizkor 31
Yocheved 19
Yom Kippur 31

Zilpa 12, 66, 68